Tamora Pierce

WHO WROTE THAT?

Tamora Pierce

Donna Dailey

Foreword by
Kyle Zimmer

CHELSEA HOUSE
PUBLISHERS
An imprint of Infobase Publishing

Tamora Pierce

Copyright © 2006 by Infobase Publishing

Chelsea House
An imprint of Infobase Publishing
132 West 31st Street
New York NY 10001

Library of Congress Cataloging-in-Publication Data

Dailey, Donna.
  Tamora Pierce / Donna Dailey.
     p. cm. — (Who wrote that?)
  Includes bibliographical references and index.
  ISBN 0-7910-8795-6
  1. Pierce, Tamora—Juvenile literature. 2. Authors, American—20th
century—Biography—Juvenile literature. 3. Children's stories—Authorship—
Juvenile
literature. I. Title. II. Series.
  PS3566.I395Z65 2005
  813'.54—dc22

Text and cover design by Keith Trego

Printed in the United States of America

Bang EJB 10 9 8 7 6 5 4 3 2 1

This book is printed on acid-free paper.

Table of Contents

HUMANITY IS POWERED by stories. From our earliest days as thinking beings, we employed every available tool to tell each other stories. We danced, drew pictures on the walls of our caves, spoke, and sang. All of this extraordinary effort was designed to entertain, recount the news of the day, explain natural occurrences—and then gradually to build religious and cultural traditions and establish the common bonds and continuity that eventually formed civilizations. Stories are the most powerful force in the universe; they are the primary element that has distinguished our evolutionary path.

Our love of the story has not diminished with time. Enormous segments of societies are devoted to the art of storytelling. Book sales in the United States alone topped $26 billion last year; movie studios spend fortunes to create and promote stories; and the news industry is more pervasive in its presence than ever before.

There is no mystery to our fascination. Great stories are magic. They can introduce us to new cultures, or remind us of the nobility and failures of our own, inspire us to greatness or scare us to death; but above all, stories provide human insight on a level that is unavailable through any other source. In fact, stories connect each of us to the rest of humanity not just in our own time, but also throughout history.

This special magic of books is the greatest treasure that we can hand down from generation to generation. In fact, that spark in a child that comes from books became the motivation for the creation of my organization, First Book, a national literacy program with a simple mission: to provide new books to the most disadvantaged children. At present, First Book has been at work in hundreds of communities for over a decade. Every year children in need receive millions of books through our organization and millions more are provided through dedicated literacy institutions across the United States and around the world. In addition, groups of people dedicate themselves tirelessly to working with children to share reading and stories in every imaginable setting from schools to the streets. Of course, this Herculean effort serves many important goals. Literacy translates to productivity and employability in life and many other valid and even essential elements. But at the heart of this movement are people who love stories, love to read, and want desperately to ensure that no one misses the wonderful possibilities that reading provides.

When thinking about the importance of books, there is an overwhelming urge to cite the literary devotion of great minds. Some have written of the magnitude of the importance of literature. Amy Lowell, an American poet, captured the concept when she said, "Books are more than books. They are the life, the very heart and core of ages past, the reason why men lived and worked and died, the essence and quintessence of their lives." Others have spoken of their personal obsession with books, as in Thomas Jefferson's simple statement: "I live for books." But more compelling, perhaps, is the almost instinctive excitement in children for books and stories.

Throughout my years at First Book, I have heard truly extraordinary stories about the power of books in the lives of children. In one case, a homeless child, who had been bounced from one location to another, later resurfaced—and the only possession that he had fought to keep was the book he was given as part of a First Book distribution months earlier. More recently, I met a child who, upon receiving the book he wanted, flashed a big smile and said, "This is my big chance!" These snapshots reveal the true power of books and stories to give hope and change lives.

As these children grow up and continue to develop their love of reading, they will owe a profound debt to those volunteers who reached out to them—a debt that they may repay by reaching out to spark the next generation of readers. But there is a greater debt owed by all of us—a debt to the storytellers, the authors, who have bound us together, inspired our leaders, fueled our civilizations, and helped us put our children to sleep with their heads full of images and ideas.

WHO WROTE THAT? is a series of books dedicated to introducing us to a few of these incredible individuals. While we have almost always honored stories, we have not uniformly honored storytellers. In fact, some of the most important authors have toiled in complete obscurity throughout their lives or have been openly persecuted for the uncomfortable truths that they have laid before us. When confronted with the magnitude of their written work or perhaps the daily grind of our own, we can forget that writers are people. They struggle through the same daily indignities and dental appointments, and they experience the intense joy and bottomless despair that many of us do. Yet somehow they rise above it all to deliver a powerful thread that connects us all. It is a rare honor to have the opportunity that these books provide to share the lives of these extraordinary people. Enjoy.

Tamora Pierce takes a moment to smile for cameras during her book signing at the East Lansing Public Library in Michigan. Members of the library's teen review board (standing behind Tammy) got to meet the author and speak with her about her writing, inspirations, and life.

A World of Fantasy

ONE DAY IN THE EARLY 1990s, some homeless people in New York City's Riverside Park rescued a baby squirrel that had fallen from its nest. They took it to the Crazy Park Lady to see if she could help. She was short and round, with short reddish-blonde hair and blue eyes behind clear-rimmed glasses. She always dressed simply in T-shirts, jeans, and tennis shoes, and she wore funny bandanas with skulls and cross-bones on them.

She was often seen in the park, feeding the squirrels and sparrows and blue jays, even when it was raining. The animals

Tamora Pierce has spent a lot of time with the animals in New York City's Riverside Park. She has always felt more at home with nature and animals than she has with crowds of people.

would come right up to her, and what's more, she talked to them and gave them names. She took the baby squirrel home with her, and kept him for a week until she found a rehabilitation center where he would be raised with other young squirrels.

The Crazy Park Lady is the author Tamora Pierce, or Tammy as she is called by her friends. And while she may use that phrase to describe herself, in fact there is nothing crazy about her bond with animals. Around the time she became a full-time author, she started going frequently to Riverside Park, which is near her home, to observe the wildlife. Visiting the park became her form of meditation. She found feeding the squirrels and birds soothing, and it took her mind off the troubles that come with being a struggling writer. Her visits to the park inspired her to create one of her finest heroines. And some of the best characters in her books are animals.

Tammy has written 23 young-adult fantasy novels, many short stories, articles, and plays that were performed on the radio. Most of her novels have been recorded as audio books. And she has at least seven more books planned over the next five years. All of her novels have one thing in common: they feature strong female characters that, in her words, "kick butt."

Tammy was born in 1954 in a small town in western Pennsylvania's coal-mining country, South Connellsville. She began writing at the age of 11, when her father heard her telling herself stories as she washed the dishes, and suggested she start writing them down. From that moment, she never looked back, writing continually, in one form or another, throughout her teenage and college years. A few months after graduation from the University of Pennsylvania, she completed her first novel, *The Song of the Lioness*, originally written for adults.

For three years Pierce had no luck finding a publisher who would publish her work. Her break came when she moved to New York City and an agent at the literary agency where she worked recommended she turn *The Song of the Lioness* into a series of four books for teenagers. And so, almost by accident, Tammy began writing for young adults; her early books all appeared as quartets.

Tammy's first novel, *Alanna: The First Adventure*, was

published in autumn 1983. Nearly two decades later, in August 2002, her 19th book, *Lady Knight*, debuted at number one on the *New York Times* list of best-selling children's books. It also hit number six on the *Wall Street Journal* general fiction list, a list that includes adult fiction. (The previous children's writer to make that list was J.K. Rowling.) In 2004, Tammy's novel *Trickster's Queen* stayed on the *New York Times* bestseller list for seven weeks.

Although Tammy's books did not receive the headline-splashing, overnight success that has characterized much of children's literature in recent years, her books have never been out of print. From the very beginning, *Alanna: The First Adventure* sold steadily. Her novels have been printed in other languages and have sold over four million copies worldwide.

Tammy's love of fantasy and adventure stories began in early childhood. She likes to say that as the first-born of three girls, she was her father's oldest son. From her first hero, Robin Hood, she grew up reading what were considered "boy books"—swashbucklers such as *The Three Musketeers* by Alexandre Dumas, action stories like *Treasure Island* by Robert Louis Stevenson, and novels about King Arthur and his knights. She lapped up world myths and legends, westerns by Zane Grey, J.R.R. Tolkien's *Lord of the Rings* trilogy, and all the fantasy and science fiction she could find.

But there were very few female warriors or heroes in the books she loved. Tammy thought the writers had simply forgotten to include girls, so she began to write about them. From the start, she wrote in the style of the stories she liked to read. She based her writing on her favorite books and television programs. She wrote about time travel, space exploration, and great battles; she wrote action-packed stories with brave, teenage-girls doing great deeds and commanding fantastic magic—all the things she wished she could do.

Tammy's fictional world is full of fearless girl warriors, powerful mages (magic-workers), healers, and clever

Did you know...

Tamora Pierce observes that fantasy fans are often very intense people; they are also very intelligent, very demanding, and very perceptive. She said:

> To fulfill that audience's expectations you have to be as real as possible because they won't be satisfied with anything less. The best fantasy writers, the ones that I enjoy, have a depth of emotion and passion and reality in their writing . . . . Good fantasy writers will give you as much a burst of human experience in one book as they can fit in. They understand the readership has that need for the real world in fantasy . . . . People look at speculative fiction, which includes science fiction and horror as well as fantasy, and say, well, it's all made up. The best fantasy is always thoroughly rooted in reality. When I speak about writing, I try to break down that wall of prejudice, and show how authors draw on real-world things to give their fantasy novels heft and meaning and power.*

* Donna Dailey's interviews with Tamora Pierce, May–July 2005.

animals that seem almost human. There are immortal gods and goddesses, mythical dragons and griffins, and fantastical creatures called Coldfangs, Stormwings, spidrens, and krakens. These are not simply the products of a marvelous imagination. Everything Tammy writes is rooted in the real world, inspired by history, mythology, religion, and social customs of many different cultures.

"Fantasy doesn't work unless it's real," Tammy said. "If it's all made up and fluffy, it's immensely unsatisfying."[1] In researching material for her books, she has studied martial arts and magic, read up on military history, learned to spin wool, and consulted a female jouster at a Renaissance fair.

If you talk to Tammy for any length of time, two things stand out: her phenomenal memory and her life-long love of writing. She can still recall each kind of paper and writing implement she used at different stages of her writing life, from the chafing of her fingers during her pencil phase, to her lined manila paper and black pen phase, to her graph paper and purple, fiber-point pen phase.

Writing served another purpose in her early years. It helped her block out the pain of a troubled childhood in which she suffered poverty, her parents' divorce, and life with an abusive mother. The family moved around a lot, from a conservative, rural area of Pennsylvania to a more liberal area of California and back again. Each time they moved from house to house, their financial problems worsened. For much of her youth, Tammy felt like a geek who did not fit in with the rest of society, and because of that she became something of a loner. Writing kept her sane and it became her way of dealing with the world.

Even when things were at their darkest, Tammy found good things to balance the bad. She said:

I've been lucky in that every place I've lived, I've been able to find beauty there. And that really meant a lot to me. There were always good books, and friends, and special places that I still remember as vividly as the bad stuff, moments of pure enjoyment, out in nature, when I was overwhelmed with wonder. I can also name books for certain periods that just caught me up and took me over.[2]

Through sheer love of the genre, Tammy stuck to writing fantasy, even when her family and teachers discouraged her. Pursuing her interests has led not only to deep personal fulfillment but also to literary success. As a teenager she learned that you must write about things you like. "If you're not happy writing it," she said, "people won't be happy reading it."[3]

Tammy believes fantasy is a powerful and passionate literature that speaks directly to the soul of readers because nearly everyone has grown up listening to and reading fairy tales. Fantasy has a basic vocabulary readers can share. It talks openly about issues of honor and glory, duty and responsibility, both to those who lead you and to those you lead. Fantasy focuses on the heroism of one person or many, and shows how they can make a difference.

Books changed Tammy's life when she was a child, and because of that she finds it rewarding to write for teenagers and pre-teens. "Girls of that age are idealistic, eager, and devoted," she said. "They want something great and grand to latch on to, and I love seeing that in their faces."[4] She enjoys meeting her fans at bookstore appearances, and speaking at schools and libraries. She founded the Sheroes Central website with author Meg Cabot, so that girls (and boys) of all ages would have a place to come and share their female heroes and voice their opinions. Tammy told a Syracuse newspaper:

Kids in particular are the least empowered citizens of our culture, and fantasy with magic gives me a believable way to give kids power. And a way to come at extremely important issues that don't get discussed openly.[5]

In her storylines, Tammy tackles problems that children must face in the real world, such as crime, illness, loneliness, bullying, and natural disasters. She does not shy away from the topics of sex and violence, because she knows that many teenagers deal with those issues in their own lives. She is particularly good at describing the first feelings of attraction between girls and boys, wonderful and overwhelming at the same time, and those early feelings of uncertainty. Fans often say that Tammy's characters are so realistic they seem like people they know.

Many of the romantic relationships in her books— Alanna and George, or Daine and Numair—are based on a man who loves a woman who many men find difficult or disturbing simply because she is unique and does not fit into a woman's stereotypical role. Such love and happy endings are not just found in fantasy books; despite coming from a broken home, Tammy has found happiness and harmony in her own marriage. She once said in an autobiographical sketch:

I write about people who cut their own deal with life, shaping their futures to fit their unique skills and outlooks. That is the approach to life that worked for me and for those I respect, and from what my readers tell me in their letters, that is the point of view they take away from my books.[6]

From her office on New York's Upper West Side, surrounded by the books, maps, and photos she uses to create her fictional worlds, Tammy makes writing seem like the most fun job in the world. But before she got to where she is today, there were many years of hard work and worry, and a life as dramatic, clever, and determined as any of her heroines.

Tamora Pierce was born in South Connellsville, a town in western Pennsylvania that was well known for its coal mining industry. This photo was taken after the Red Lion coal mining strike in a neighboring town a few years before Tammy was born.

Country Girl

ON DECEMBER 13, 1954, a nurse in South Connellsville, Pennsylvania presented a young couple with their first child. The dark-haired parents were somewhat shocked to see their baby girl had a tuft of bright red hair, brushed up and tied with a pink bow.

The baby's mother wanted to call her daughter Tamara, but in the Pennsylvania coal country of the 1950s, the nurse had never heard of such an unusual name. When she filled out the birth certificate she misspelled it, and the baby became Tamora Pierce (rhymes with "camera").

For years the family teased Tammy's mother about giving birth to the only redhead they knew. The mystery of baby Tamora's fiery hair was explained a few years later, when her father grew a moustache that was the same red color. Only then did the relatives remember that Tammy's father-had been a redhead as a young boy.

Tammy was born into a long, proud line of people who had deep routs in western Pennsylvania's Appalachian mountains region. Her father, Wayne Franklin Pierce, was named for two heroes of the American Revolution, General Anthony Wayne and Benjamin Franklin. Wayne's ancestors had settled in the Appalachian mountains of western Pennsylvania before the War of Independence (1775–1783). Jacqueline Sparks, Tammy's mother, came from a family of Scots-Presbyterians who had immigrated to the area from Scotland in 1745.

After serving in the Korean War, Wayne studied at a university in Pittsburgh, Pennsylvania, where he met Jackie, who was a student nurse. They married soon after, when he was 24 and she was 19. Tammy was born a year and a half later.

Wayne had intense blue eyes and black hair that turned a beautiful heavy silver color as he aged. He had a stocky build and stood about five feet, nine inches tall. In his later years he wore a short beard. Tammy loved his voice best, a deep, smoky baritone that spoke with a strong country accent. Jackie was a slender five feet, seven inches, with brown hair, brown eyes, and freckles. She was an attractive woman, with high cheekbones, a long nose, and a thin mouth. When she dressed up, Tammy thought she was very elegant.

From an early age, Tammy was inspired by her father's keen interest in history. As a boy, Wayne and his brother

Lysle explored the mountains in their corner of south west Pennsylvania, stumbling across old one-mule mines and abandoned family graveyards. They were the two youngest members of the Pennsylvania Historical Society.

Tammy's maternal grandfather shared Wayne's enthusiasm. One night Clyde Sparks, Sr. called Wayne to say he had something very interesting to show him. While surveying the land to build a new road through the mountains, they had discovered the true location of Fort Necessity, George Washington's first command in the French and Indian War. The excavations revealed where guns had been buried under the walls to keep them from the enemy.

From the beginning, Tammy was surrounded by a rich family of storytellers. "My dad could tell a story so you felt you were in it," she recalled. "You could live through the Revolution or the Civil War with him just as easily as Korea or anything he'd done in his own life."[7]

Most of Tammy's relatives lived nearby in Fayette County, and they would often gather for big family picnics. As everyone relaxed after dessert, Uncle Lysle, Aunt Betty, or Aunt Irene would start talking about their lives when they were kids, and soon there was a river of stories from the family that carried Tammy along. "Till the end of his life, my dad would just start talking and you'd be carried along on that same great tide," she said. "Even my mother, if you got her going, could make any incident from her life into something just as riveting as a good book."[8]

When Tammy was 5 years old, her sister Kimberly was born and the family moved to the small town of Dunbar, Pennsylvania. A year later, her youngest sister, Melanie, arrived. Their two-story house had inexpensive composite siding—man made from shredded wood, sawdust, or a cement product—and a coal furnace in the basement. Tammy was not allowed to go down to the basement, but she can still summon up the scent of that furnace.

Did you know...

"Hillbillies" is a term used to describe the people who came to America and settled in the Appalachian mountain area that stretches from western Pennsylvania through Virginia, West Virginia, Kentucky, and Tennessee on down into the Ozarks in Missouri. By and large, hillbillies are of Irish, German, and Scottish ancestry—many are descended from Scottish clans who were evicted from their lands following a failed rebellion against the English in 1745 (the Appalachians reminded them of their own Highlands).

Real hillbillies are not at all like the caricatures portrayed in television shows. According to Tamora Pierce, they are a strong, independent, and often stubborn people, who would rather be poor than take charity. Pride is very important. Hillbillies work hard to make a living and they are notorious for their dislike of the government or anyone sticking their nose into someone else's business. They are certainly not stupid. Many are readers and crafters, people who make things. While they may be poor, they make the most of what they have. To them, family is most important, and they will do whatever it takes to protect each other; they share what they can and help each other out whenever possible.

Water was mechanically pumped in from a well, and Tammy used to drop pebbles through the hole in the well cover just to hear them "clink" far below.[9]

The family was poor, but Tammy did not know it then. Everyone in Dunbar lived a similar lifestyle. Seven years later, when she saw the town again, it looked dinky and run-down, contradicting her happy childhood memories.

There was half an acre of land in back of the house, with a flower garden and a big tree where she dug looking for pirate treasure. They had a pear tree and Concord grape vines. Wayne kept homing pigeons in a pigeon coop, and they always had pet cats and dogs. In the summer, Tammy's parents made their own root beer. Jackie canned everything that came out of the family's big vegetable garden—straw-berries, green beans, corn. She made bread and butter pick-les from cucumbers and ketchup from the tomatoes.

The house had a sunny kitchen with a pantry. The pantry's shelves were always stocked with dried fruit and canned goods. While her mother did the cooking and iron-ing, Tammy learned to do the dishes. She had her own room, which looked out over the porch, with a wooden toy chest big enough for her to curl up and hide in. When she was unable to sleep at night, she made up her own stories about the popular television characters from the show *Rin Tin Tin*.

Wayne worked as a lineman for the Bell Telephone Com-pany. He hated being indoors. Jackie wanted to become a teacher and went to college for her English degree. Nowa-days, many mothers work or pursue their education outside the home, but in small-town Pennsylvania in the 1960s, it was an unusual occurrence. Wayne always supported Jackie in her studies, and the children were cared for by a babysit-ter when she was in class. The babysitter indulged Tammy's

Tamora Pierce's first hero was Robin Hood, the legendary character who made his home in England's Sherwood Forest. Pictured here is a large tree known as the Major Oak, which stands in Sherwood Forest near Edwinstowe, Nottinghamshire, England. Legend has it that Robin Hood hid from his enemies inside the Major Oak. Tammy was excited when she was able to visit the site on a Scholastic-sponsored tour in 2000 to promote The Circle Opens quartet.

early love of adventure stories and let her watch *Robin Hood* on television before she went to school. If Jackie was home, the television was tuned to *Captain Kangaroo* for Kimberly and Melanie, no matter how much Tammy pleaded to see her favorite hero.

Tammy's home was atypical in other ways, too. It was filled with weird artifacts, such as African masks and a fake shrunken head Wayne had found. There were Chinese figurines and a laughing Buddha which they always kept with them, rubbing his belly for luck. The house had cracks in the light-green walls and ceiling which they could not afford to repair, so Jackie painted the cracks dark green to look like a vine growing through the living room.

There were always plenty of books in the house. Uncle Bob, Jackie's brother, gave Tammy the first books of her very own, a four-book set of A.A. Milne works, including *Winnie the Pooh*. He also gave the family a set of World Book Encyclopedias. Even before Tammy could read, she loved to leaf through the encyclopedias, looking at the pictures. Tammy's parents always shared their adult books with the children, and let them look at anything they wanted. The only rules were that they had to wash their hands before touching the books and they had to sit on the couch while looking at them.

Jackie's art books from college provided more fertile territory for the inquisitive 5-year-old. One day, Jackie saw Tammy heading for the couch with *Janson's History of Art*. The book was full of pictures of classical works, with nude statues and paintings. When she heard Tammy call, she figured she would have some explaining to do, especially when she saw that the book was open to a full-page plate of Michelangelo's statue, *David*. To her relief, Tammy just pointed to the naked figure and said, "Mum, that man is barefooted."[10]

Most of the books were kept in the dining room, which was Tammy's favorite room in the house. Here, each December, usually on her birthday, Wayne would put up a big plywood table and set up his model train set. The track was surrounded by a miniature village, and every year Jackie would get him a new piece to add to it.

They worked on the setup together. Jackie painted the farmhouse to make it look old and added vines that looked like they were growing on the sides of the church. She made a mountain covered with trees and a tunnel for the train to run through. Wayne wired all the little houses for lights, and made them look so lived-in that Tammy could imagine the people inside. There were chickens in the farmyard, a Model A car with a rumble seat, and even an outhouse with a man in red long-johns running out to it. It was a real work of art. People came from miles around to see it, while Tammy hid underneath the table listening to them talk.

Tammy went happily off to kindergarten, then first grade at Dunbar Elementary, a little red brick schoolhouse. Her wavy red hair had softened into strawberry blonde, and she wore it in a tight braid. She quickly learned to read, and by second grade she was delving into the World Book Encyclopedia at last. In third grade, after a fast bout of measles followed by chicken pox, Tammy returned to school unable to see the blackboard. She hated her new blue-frame glasses, and felt like the ultimate girl geek.

During the summer months, Tammy's parents would make bags of popcorn and take their children to the drive-in movies. Tammy usually fell asleep, but her parents made sure to wake her in time to see the chariot race in *Ben Hur*.

Other times, the family took long drives up into the mountains by Fort Necessity or the Ohiopyle Falls Waterfall in Ohiopyle State Park, Pennsylvania. As night was drawing down, her parents would sing folk songs, spirituals, and country songs, Wayne's baritone harmonizing with Jackie's lyric soprano. Tammy loved those long summer drives, with the cool night air and the sound of the tree frogs coming in the windows. She felt safe and protected in the back seat, listening to her parents sing.

When Tammy's parents were connected, she felt there was nothing they could not withstand. But soon they would embark on a very different journey, and their happy life in western Pennsylvania would seem very far away.

When Tamora Pierce was 8 years old, her family packed up their belongings in their Volkswagen van and moved to California. Camping along the way, Tammy saw and experienced America for the first time.

3

The First Adventure

IN MAY 1963, JACKIE PIERCE got her college degree in English. Eight-year-old Tammy proudly attended her mother's graduation ceremony. At the time, Wayne Pierce had itchy feet and wanted to see new places. Now that Jackie had her teaching certificate the time seemed right for a change. Wayne arranged a job transfer with the telephone company, and in June, the family packed up and moved to California.

The Pierce family drove cross-country in a Volkswagen bus, camping out along the way. The children slept in the bus, while their parents pitched a tent outside. In a marshlands campground in Missouri, Tammy saw her first water lilies and egrets (a type of long-legged wading bird), but the two-week journey with two toddlers and a lot of bugs put Tammy off camping for life. Soaked in mosquito repellent, she soon dropped her childish habit of sucking her thumb. In Kansas they encountered sandstorms. At a Colorado Springs campground, Tammy went to experience her first shower in the wild, only to discover—much too late for comfort—that the water was ice cold. Worst of all, she found she could not read on the road because it made her car sick. Tammy was completely bored.

Finally they arrived in California. Tammy met her Uncle Bob for the first time in San Bruno. She and her sisters stayed with him and Aunt Susan for two weeks while her parents went house-hunting. Tammy found she did not much like the man who had given them their beloved encyclopedias. He teased her, and he and Aunt Susan were strict with the three children. Tammy was glad when her own parents returned.

The Pierce's first house was nearby in San Mateo. They had to sleep on the floor until their furniture arrived. At first, it all seemed very strange to Tammy. Apart from the long journey, she had looked forward to being in California. It was the land of opportunity.

"It was going to be this cool adventure," she recalled. "And then we got there, and it was so different from anything we'd ever known."[11]

Tammy started fourth grade. She was of average height and weight for her age, with a short pixie haircut, but she felt like an oddball. Compared to the other kids, she dressed funny, she wore her hair funny, and she talked funny. Everything else was alien and so was she. She could not put her finger on exactly why she was different from the other kids; she just knew she was.

That November, Tammy was outside at recess when a classmate told her that the president, John F. Kennedy, had been shot. Back in the classroom the teachers brought in a television to watch the tragic news. It was the first time Tammy had felt jolted by the outside world. To her, it was like an immense earthquake, as if a god had fallen. Her teachers, parents, the whole country, it seemed, had gone silent as they struggled to come to terms with what had happened.

Tammy did her best to fit in, but soon the family moved again. Miramar, California, was a tiny fishing town on the other side of the peninsula near Half Moon Bay, down the coast from San Francisco. Once again, for the second half of her fourth grade year, Tammy was the new kid in school.

Here, the teachers—and eventually Tammy herself—realized she was smart. She gave the right answers in class, and talked about books that her classmates would not read for a long time yet. By now she was eagerly reading her mother's Golden Books of Greek myths and legends. When a fellow student said she used "big words," Tammy pointed out that "azure" is actually a very short word. Soon she got the nickname "Walking Encyclopedia."[12]

Tammy liked living by the ocean. She flew kites, and went out to watch the surfers at sunset. One night, as the fog rolled in, her father read Edgar Allan Poe's *The Raven* out loud as the foghorns blew in the distance.

Her parents found a tiny beach called Arroyo de los Frijoles, or "Bean Hollow." It had a deadly riptide, so it was not a place they could swim, but they would take the children there at minus tide, when the tide went out for about half a mile. Then they could walk out among the exposed rocks, exploring the tidal pools. In the hollows and trenches and cracks in the rocks, Tammy found new worlds normally covered by salt water, and teeming with sea urchins, limpets, hermit crabs, and other creatures. She was amazed by their hidden lives.

Tammy loved going to Bean Hollow, despite the early start necessary to catch the minus tide—they had to be there with the dawn. Her parents cooked breakfast on the beach, on a cookie sheet over an open fire. Even with the sand in it, the food tasted so much better than it would have at home.

Nearby was an even smaller pebble beach, its stones all tumbled and smoothed by the waves. Tammy would scoop up a handful of the rock and find tiny pieces of tiger eye, perfectly formed miniature seashells and bits of colored glass rounded by the sea. It was like scooping up a handful of treasure.

But beneath these happy times was the undercurrent of her parents' arguing. They moved around a lot because they often could not pay the rent. California was expensive, and one job did not provide enough to cover their expenses. Without a second car, it was hard for Jackie to get a job and keep it. It was in Miramar that Tammy first noticed her mother drinking. When anyone asked her mother why she had begun to drink, her mom would say that she had a pinched nerve and the wine dulled the pain.

In June they moved to El Granada, California, a slightly bigger town up the coast. Tammy knew kids from school there, and she went to summer recreation activities. She spent much of her time in the local library. After attending fifth grade here, the family moved again across the peninsula to Burlingame, on San Francisco Bay.

For the past year, her parents' marriage had been fraying

badly. Twice, her mother had packed a suitcase and threatened to leave. In Burlingame, things got worse and the fighting became physical.

For reasons Tammy would never figure out, her mother's mental health was deteriorating. She looked for reasons to pick a fight, and if she could not find an excuse she would make one. Wayne had a short fuse, but he coped as well as anybody could with a woman who was becoming increasingly violent. Jackie made Tammy think it was her father who was the abusive one, but years later, when Tammy was able to look back objectively at their fights, she realized it was always a case of her father restraining her mother. By his code, a man did not let a woman hit him, but a man did not hit a woman either. Jackie tried to make him do something she knew he would hate himself for. He was a battered husband at a time when it was shameful to talk about it.

Jackie blamed everyone but herself for not rising higher in life. She applied for jobs she was not qualified for, then claimed the male establishment was against her because she was female. She always had an excuse to reject the jobs she could do. As she became more and more discouraged she began drinking all the time, and when she drank she hit people, including her own children if they argued with her. But Wayne was always Jackie's first target. When they were fighting, Tammy and her sisters would hide and pray that their parents would patch up their marriage, but they did not. They could not.

One evening, when Tammy was in sixth grade, Wayne heard her telling herself stories while she did the dishes. He suggested that she start writing them down. She knew he was serious when he said she could even use his typewriter. Since she had been forbidden to touch the typewriter until then, this told her how important her writing was to him.

Tammy adored her father and would have done anything he asked, so she gave it a try.

Wayne suggested Tammy write a book about travels in a

Did you know...

As soon as she learned to read, Tamora Pierce looked up her old television hero, Robin Hood, in the encyclopedia. It contained cross-references to the Crusades and Richard the Lionheart, so she read about them, too. For the next four years she read everything she could find, both fiction and nonfiction, about knights, the Crusades, and the Middle Ages.

This was followed by her mythology period. Tammy read about the ancient Egyptians, Greek and Roman myths, and Norse myths.

In middle school she turned to the legends about King Arthur. She read *The Once and Future King* by T.H. White and Mary Stewart's *The Crystal Cave*. After her introduction to J.R.R. Tolkien's trilogy, *Lord of the Rings*, she delved into fantasy: Robert Howard's *Conan*, Michael Moorcock's Elric stories, and books by E.R. Edison.

Her father introduced her to the novels of Edgar Rice Burroughs, creator of Tarzan, and she also read old swashbuckling books by Raphael Sabatini, westerns by Zane Grey, historical fiction by Samuel Shellabarger, and books about James Bond by Ian Fleming. In ninth grade Tammy discovered science fiction and the works of Isaac Asimov, Ray Bradbury, and Robert Heinlein.

time machine. They both liked history, and enjoyed television programs such as *Star Trek*, so he knew time travel would capture her attention. Tammy had been reading about the fall of Troy in ancient Greece, and also about the pirate Blackbeard. She put all of the things she would have liked to see for herself into her stories. Instead of making everything up, she used herself and kids she knew as characters.

Tammy found she loved writing. She could not tell a story out loud as well as her father could, but she was teaching herself to do it on paper. More importantly, writing gave her a way to escape the unpleasantness at home. Reading and writing became her mainstays ever after. Her fictional world gave her control and a way to fight back. It rendered life at home more tolerable.

Unfortunately, Jackie knew where her daughter's urge to write came from, and she did not like it. It became a source of real animosity between them. Jackie felt that writing took Tammy away from her, and she found subtle ways to make Tammy feel bad about herself and her writing. Tammy knew her mother was smart and looked to her for approval, but she could not understand why her writing made her mother angry.

Mrs. Jacobsen was Tammy's seventh grade English teacher and homeroom advisor. She knew about Tammy's troubles at home and helped her as much as she could. Mrs. Jacobsen introduced Tammy to the Lord of the Rings trilogy by J.R.R. Tolkien. Tammy was fascinated, and plunged into Tolkien's complex world of epic fantasy, and other sword and sorcery novels. At the end of the school year, Mrs. Jacobsen moved to Chicago. Tammy was heartbroken.

Luckily, every year there was at least one teacher who supported Tammy and her interests. These teachers made it clear that they thought she had something to offer and would

While in middle-school, Tamora Pierce took a teacher's suggestion that she read novels by author J.R.R. Tolkien. The sorcery and magic in Tolkien's Lord of the Rings trilogy captured Tammy's attention and sparked her imagination. This portrait of Tolkien was taken in the 1940s.

eventually make her mark in the world. Tammy always made friends with librarians, who would talk with her about books and suggest some of their favorites. Other adults in school clubs and youth programs agreed that Tammy was smart and encouraged her to write and act. These outside positive influences helped Tammy balance the negativity associated with going home to her mother, whom Tammy loved and respected, but who whittled away at her self esteem.

On Mother's Day in 1966, Wayne moved out. Jackie called his leaving "her present to herself," which left Tammy with ambiguous feelings. Jackie had taken her daughters out for the day, and when they came home, all of Wayne's things were gone. Even though Tammy had sensed it was coming, his leaving was pretty hard to take. Jackie told her children that they would just have to get used to it.

That summer, Tammy started acting at a recreational children's theater. But as soon as she started to enjoy herself, her mother came and pulled her out, saying she was needed at home to watch her sisters. The teachers talked to Jackie and told her that Tammy was good at acting and that she needed to do it. They asked her to let Tammy stay. Jackie relented, but she was not happy about it.

At the theater, Tammy met Mike Dilts. He was two years older than she and, like Tammy, was also into mythology and fantasy books. He introduced her to books by Michael Moorcock.

Tammy did not realize it for a long time, but it was her first courtship. Mike had invented an Orkish alphabet for Tolkien, and he would leave letters for Tammy in the mailbox attached to their flagpole. As he pedaled away furiously on his bicycle, Tammy's sisters ran after him shouting "TP plus MD."[13] They even wrote it on the wall of the local grocery store. Tammy thought she would die of embarrassment. She and Mike traded letters back and forth about mythology, Tolkien, and the fantasy books they were reading. He was the first friend who shared her interests. It was wonderful.

All the while, Tammy was writing stories. Sometimes she used characters and settings from her favorite books and television programs. Other times she created everything from scratch, leaning heavily toward fantasy or science fiction themes. Often her stories mirrored the kind of books she was reading at that moment, but with one major difference: the books she loved lacked teenage-girl heroes, so Tammy wrote about her own girl warriors. She made these girls brave, bold, and athletic—all the things she herself desperately wanted to be.

Tammy's mother made it clear she did not like her daughter's writing. An English literature major through and through, Jackie did not approve of science fiction and fantasy, or of the comic books Tammy was also devouring. She called such books "that junk."

Once Tammy showed her mother a fantasy story she had written. It was full of armies and combat with swords and spears. Her mother read it and dismissed it with a critical word. Tammy went to her room and took out a large box of work. It was full of writing ideas and scraps of stories she had started and never finished. She picked up each and every page, and tore it into little pieces. Tammy has never stopped regretting losing those pieces.

Even after that incident Tammy did not give up. Writing was not only interesting to her, it also served another purpose. It helped her block out the painful drama of her parents' long, drawn-out divorce.

Tammy wanted to live with her father. Wayne had visitation rights, but Jackie made sure it was a fight every time, and Tammy was getting increasingly terrible stomach aches with each argument. In December, Tammy was away for a weekend when her sister called and said that their mother was sick and had bruised her. Tammy went back home to find that her mother had been drinking and was passed out on the couch. When Jackie awoke, they had a dreadful fight. Tammy was injured and ran away to her father's place.

Wayne was renting a room from a woman who also worked at the phone company. Her name was Mary Lou; she was Tammy's future stepmother. Tammy knew right away that Mary Lou was the person her father should have married.

Jackie got a court order to get Tammy back. At the hearing, Tammy begged to go with her father. When she told them the things her mother had done, they put her and her sisters into a group foster home for a couple of weeks until their case could be heard again.

During the time they were living in the foster home, Tammy tried to look after her sisters while she also dealt with her mother and the social services system. The social workers heard her telling stories to amuse her roommates at night. Later Tammy found out they had said she should be put in a psychiatric ward for observation. Learning this did not help her feel safe at all.

Jackie swore to the court that she had stopped drinking. She cleaned up the dirty house, and got rid of all the liquor. When the hearing came, as Tammy told the court the things her mother had done, she realized they did not believe her, perhaps thinking this was just another one of her stories. She gave up. She knew the court had already made up their minds: Tammy and her sisters were going back to live with their mother.

The court required them to see a social worker, so Jackie behaved better for a while. However, eventually she went back to drinking and abusing everyone around her. Tammy still saw her father on visitation nights, but now there was no way they would be going to live with him. So she tried to look after her sisters as best she could, without having any idea how to do it.

This picture of Tamora Pierce (standing) and the Uniontown Senior High cast of the play "Take Her, She's Mine" was taken in 1972. The sudden move from California back to Pennsylvania was hard on young Tammy but she found solace and joy in acting in plays and writing for the school newspaper.

4

Back Home Again

BY THE TIME TAMMY STARTED high school, she and her family were living on welfare. It felt like salt in a wound.

The Monday before Thanksgiving, Tammy's father, Wayne, came and took her out of school. He had offered to pay their way back to Pennsylvania, where it would be cheaper for them to live, and Jackie had accepted. They were taking the train that very day.

Tammy was in shock. She did not have a chance to say good-bye to her friends. They had to leave their dog, which had been with them for several years, and their other pets behind. They had to leave most of their things. Behind Tammy's bed was a six-foot-tall bookcase full of books, and she could not take any of them.

Wayne and Jackie had never asked their daughters how they felt about making a move before, but this time the girls were uprooted out of the blue. Tammy was blindsided. Being shipped off like that, away from her father, who was her only source of comfort while living with her mother, was a very isolating experience. She was leaving everything she knew, and she was incredibly bitter and furious.

Tammy's sisters were just bewildered. Jackie made Tammy look after them and kept to herself for most of the long train journey. Tammy had her notebooks, and thought she could write part of the way, but the motion of the train made her sick just as she had been in the van heading to California. Once again she was utterly bored for the journey across the country. In Chicago they hit freezing weather, but they were still dressed for California. The trip affected Tammy's inner ear, and for a week afterwards, every time she put her foot down, it felt like the floor came up in a rocking motion.

They arrived in Pennsylvania on Thanksgiving Day. The Prices—Uncle Bud and Aunt Irene, Wayne's sister—took them in for a couple of weeks. They bought clothes and furniture, and even co-signed a loan for a car. Jackie's family was ashamed that she had left her husband. (In the late 1960s in western Pennsylvania divorce was not common.) They wanted nothing to do with her, but the Pierces and the Prices got them on their feet, and welcomed them back to the family of uncles, aunts, and cousins.

While in California Tammy remembered Pennsylvania fondly and throughout the trip back east she had tried to look forward to that aspect, at least. But when she saw Dunbar and Connellsville, she found them very different from her memories. Now the towns seemed small and dirty. Jackie told her that it had always been that way. The disappointment made the move even worse.

Jackie found a house in Uniontown, about 10 blocks from her relatives. Once again, the house had a coal furnace. Tammy was surprised to learn that school closed for the first day of deer-hunting season. Her mother explained that that was how a lot of families stretched their meat budget for the winter. It seemed to be a whole new world.

But Tammy knew things had really changed when she went to enroll in middle school. She wore her skirt about three inches above the knee, which was practically a granny gown in California in 1969. The vice principal took one look at her outfit and said "those hemlines have got to come down."[14] Tammy ended up wearing knee-length skirts. She was furious. It made her feel even more uncool. Her hair was wavy and unruly, and it would not comb into the popular style of the time. By now she was a little too plump, a little too uncoordinated, and was starting to be a little too short. She hit five foot two in seventh grade and has stayed at that height ever since.

Tammy went from the San Francisco scene of long hair, miniskirts, flower power, and rock music on the radio, to western-Pennsylvania conservatism, with its twin sets, white blouses with round collars, and pop music. There was not a hippie in sight. It was quite a culture shock. "I was an experience for them," she said, "and they were an experience for me."[15]

Tammy was put into accelerated classes. Her first friend there was Karen Datko, a vivacious girl who also had a single mother. Karen was tall and lean, with a glossy mane of straight dark hair, sparkling brown eyes, full lips, and a small

Always an eager participant in school activities, Tamora Pierce won the Voice of Democracy Award for a speech she had given. Tammy, second from left, worked hard throughout high school to overcome her family's poverty. At times writing could not be her number one priority. Nevertheless, she never stopped dreaming of becoming an author.

nose. She was fun, slightly wild, and had a lively way of talking that made Tammy laugh.

Eventually Karen became the editor of the student newspaper. Tammy wrote articles and satires for the paper. The principal found some of their humor a bit too sharp and banned the last issue. Tammy learned that things that were considered funny in California were not taken so well in western Pennsylvania. Neither did the paper's readers understand Tammy's strange views about the role of women. Like her mother, Tammy supported feminism. She was tired of being told what she could not do simply because she was female.

Tammy's family was on welfare, and she found that very hard to accept. Most of her classmates had parents with money; their clothes were more expensive, they had better haircuts, and they certainly did not have ugly glasses. Tammy continued to feel like an outcast and a loner.

At home, Tammy scrubbed clothes by hand and looked after her sisters while her mother worked night shifts as a nurse's aid. The Pierces and Prices continued to help them out. They took them ice and roller skating and to family picnics and get-togethers. Tammy learned about the Quakers in her history class, and was so intrigued that she began attending Quaker Meeting for Worship. In 1969, the tone of the meeting was very political. Messages often focused on ending the Vietnam War. Tammy really related to the members and she liked their spirit; the idea of listening within yourself for the voice of God appealed to her.

That summer Jackie got her family evicted again. The house had become so filthy that it was actually destroyed. She then found them a place on a little country road, three miles outside of nearby Smithfield, Pennsylvania. She told the children it would be "an adventure." Tammy knew her choice of words was a bad sign.

Their new home was an outbuilding on a farm, where the farmer put up the farm worker and his family. It was in a cow pasture and had two bedrooms, a kitchen, and a living room. There was a coal furnace and a well for water. The house did not have a bathroom, only an outhouse, and it did not have a bathtub. (Tammy hated having to take wash-cloth baths in the sink.)

Next door was the farmhouse owned by Mr. Dills. He lived there with his daughter Betty, a medicated schizophrenic who helped him around the farm when she was well.

Life there was hard in so many ways, but Tammy found comfort in the wonder of nature. Living out in the country, on winter nights there were no clouds and no city lights to cover up the stars, and she could see everything.

Tammy took the bus to Albert Gallatin High School, where she started 10th grade. She was still writing, and fighting with her mother about science fiction and fantasy novels. That year, she lost the ability to write her own stories.

Tammy's new teachers agreed with Jackie. They frowned on science fiction and fantasy and told her she should write about real life. One day, after attending a birthday party, she wrote a factual story about real kids at the party. She did not enjoy writing it, but she copied it all out in pencil on her best binder paper and sent it to *Seventeen* magazine.

The editor, Babette Rosmund, wrote Tammy a nice letter explaining about professional format and typing submissions before sending them. She encouraged Tammy to keep writing and sending her pieces out. Tammy appreciated that the busy woman had taken the time to help her.

When Tammy's mother saw the envelope and asked her about it, Tammy thought she would be proud. But instead Jackie flew into a rage. Her words cut Tammy to ribbons: Why did she think she was good enough to be published? All she did was write "that junk." What right did she have to send it out, she might never be published. It went on and on and on.

Tammy set out to run away. She had never worked up the courage to do anything of the kind before, or since. She started walking down the road. But she was too afraid of the world and what might happen. She knew if she went to her relatives they would only send her back. So she went home.

After that incident, Tammy found she could no longer write original fiction. She just completely dried up. She

Did you know...

Tamora Pierce began by writing J.R.R. Tolkien stories and Star Trek stories. She often put herself or her friends into those settings as characters. Today this kind of writing is called fan fiction. It is fiction written by fans using another writer's characters and universe.

Although Tammy no longer writes or reads fan fiction, she thinks it is a great way to ease yourself into writing. She said:

> Creating a whole universe or a magical system or even just a series of characters to back up your main characters can be awfully intimidating. Fan fiction is an easy way to slide into writing. It's not so overwhelming to write this way. If you are going to write for a living, you will add more and more of your own touches until sooner or later you break out and try your own thing. Even if you don't want to write professionally, you still get a lot out of it and have a lot of fun.*

There are several Websites where writers can post fan fiction, and some have followings of their own. Now Tammy's novels are the basis for many fan fiction stories. She is the third most popular author, after Tolkien and J.K. Rowling, on *www.fanfic.net*, the biggest fan fiction website.

* Donna Dailey's interviews with Tamora Pierce, May–July 2005.

could write school papers, funny essays for the school newspaper, or take-offs on fairy tales to amuse her friends. But nothing inspired her to make up her own stories.

In desperation Tammy tried writing blank verse. Jackie would go over her daughter's writing and tell her how to refit it to her literary code of iambic pentameter. Tammy tried, but by then all the fun was wrung out of it.

From that moment back in sixth grade when her father had suggested her first book, Tammy had never been without paper and pens or pencils to hand. She wrote all the time. She wrote on buses, she wrote in cars, she wrote in bed, she wrote in front of the television, she wrote everywhere. It was how she coped with the world.

Writing stories had been like breathing, so when she tried more times than she could count to write something of her own, something that was her, and it just did not and would not come, she felt as though she had lost an arm. The other things she was writing could not fulfill her. But she would not be able to write any original fiction for five more years.

Tammy had managed a couple of brief phone calls with her father after they left California. Her mother had influenced her to view him with contempt, so the calls did not go well. Then Tammy lost track of him when they moved to Smithfield. She would not renew contact with him until she was in college. Tammy admitted:

> The trouble was, when you lived with my mother, you had to see things her way. Kim never saw things her way, and I admired her courage, but my mother had me pretty well ground down by then.[16]

Despite the numerous horrible times with her mother, Tammy also had long conversations with Jackie about books, art, politics, and history. Jackie's intellect was impressive.

There was a whole other side to her, one Tammy's sisters mostly did not have a chance to see. Tammy once read something her mother had written. She thought it was incredibly good, even though it was short, but Jackie never expanded it. Jackie was so scared of failing that she never really tried to succeed.

Tammy's mother, as much as her father, shaped her intellectual world view. She learned much about the world and its workings from Jackie. That is why Tammy was confused for so long: "I knew she was brilliant. That was the reason I thought she knew what she was doing in terms of my writing, whether it was poetry or fiction."[17]

After her sophomore year, Tammy took a summer job at a tobacco camp in Massachusetts alongside other students and migrant workers. The job was to tie up the plants so they did not break under their own weight, and later to sew the plants onto slats and transport them through the barns. It was hard work. The other girls at the camp were tough and generally gave Tammy a hard time. To keep from getting beaten up for being weird, Tammy would write love poetry for some of the girls to send to their boyfriends.

After five weeks, Jackie became ill and sent for her daughter to come home. By that time, Tammy had earned enough money to buy new copies of her beloved Tolkien books which she had left behind in California.

There were no after-school programs at Tammy's rural high school, but they did have an annual talent show. In her junior year, Tammy wrote a play called "The Trials of Penelope Pureheart," a parody of the old Victorian melodramas. It won second prize. At the end of the year, Tammy tried out for the school choir. But before she could join, her family moved again.

The old farmer, Mr. Dills, had died and his daughter,

Betty, spiraled wildly downhill. She turned off the water pumps because she heard voices speaking to her from the wells, and Tammy had to haul water from the cattle troughs. Finally Betty's brother came to commit her to a psychiatric ward. When he saw the state of the house, he blew up at Jackie and evicted them.

They moved back to Uniontown into a welfare hotel where they lived in one room over two bars. While they had been living in Smithfield, Tammy's mother had had occasional work as a substitute teacher. But one night, while drinking, she had fallen asleep at the wheel and crashed the car. From that point on she no longer had a way to get to work. By the time they moved to Uniontown, she was drinking pretty much full time.

Tammy began her senior year in high school. She renewed her friendships with her old classmates from ninth grade. She joined the drama club, the chorus, and became an officer in the library club. She was also on the staff of the school paper, the *Senior High News*. Tammy wrote a humorous column, "The Interviews of Carol Curtley," in which she "interviewed" such characters as Archie the Cockroach and the Jolly Green Giant. Now that she was back in Uniontown, she was able to attend Quaker meetings again. In spite of the awful hotel room she had to return to each night, for the first time she had a life outside of her home that was hers.

Tammy's mentor that year was her humanities teacher, Margaret Emelson. She was an inspiring teacher and also directed the drama club play, "Take Her, She's Mine," in which Tammy had a leading role. Tammy enjoyed her teacher's company during and after the play rehearsals.

Mrs. Emelson had a student teacher, Warren Knisbaum, from California University of Pennsylvania, a nearby state college. Warren was tall, pale, and heavy set, with loose brown hair, sharp brown eyes, and a sarcastic smile. He wore brown suits and aviator frame glasses. Tammy developed a crush on him. They got to be friends outside of class, and met in the library to talk. Warren was also keen on science fiction, and was trying to write characters and a fictional universe with his roommate, Chris Henderson.

One night, the high school drama club went to see a play at Warren's college. Chris Henderson was in it. He was the most excruciatingly handsome man Tammy had ever laid eyes on. He had sapphire blue eyes, short brown hair and beard, red lips, and a striking profile. His costume of a leotard and tights accented his broad shoulders, narrow waist, lean hips, and musculature. After the play, Warren introduced them. The boys made fun of her clothes, which made Tammy furious.

A month later, she was surprised when Chris wanted her phone number. She had had no idea that he was interested in her. Soon, Tammy was going out with a college guy. Girls who had heartily snubbed her in school now saw this gorgeous creature, Chris, who set them all aflutter, kissing her in the halls. Payback was a wonderful thing.

But Tammy discovered that Chris's personality was not nearly so attractive as his physical appearance. He was obsessed with himself, and considered himself a great artist. Unlike Tammy, he had no sense of humor and always looked on the dark side of life. He loved making grand gestures, brooding over deep subjects, and whittling away at other people's confidence.

After three months, Tammy got tired of his games and they broke up. But the relationship had been valuable. Later, she would use his good looks and poisonous personality, his obsession with his own grandeur, as the model for the villain Duke Roger in her first novel.

After high school, Tamora Pierce left Uniontown and received a full scholar-ship to the University of Pennsylvania in Philadelphia. There she majored in psychology; she hoped to help troubled children. Pictured here is Logan Hall on the university's expansive campus.

5

An Education

AFTER GRADUATION, TAMMY was awarded a full scholarship to the University of Pennsylvania. In September 1972, she moved to Philadelphia to begin her freshman year. She knew exactly what she wanted to do.

Since the sixth grade, Tammy had meant to be a writer. But she was still unable to write her own stories, and no other kind of writing satisfied her. She decided to get a degree in psychology, and work with teenagers who had similar problems as she and her sisters.

Her friend Karen Datko became her roommate in the Hill House dormitory. They were part of what was then seen to be a daring experiment: co-ed dorms. Every other suite alternated between male and female residents. The building was a square box with very small windows, surrounded by a moat with a bridge for access. Tammy, who still loved fantasy, walked around it thinking "you could defend this place against all attackers!"[18]

Her Introduction to Psychology class combined all the first-year students into one huge class of 1,400. It was held in Irvine Auditorium. During her third week at college, Tammy met Jay Levine, a cheerful hippie from upstate New York. He had glossy, dark brown hair which fell in ringlets to his shoulders, large hazel eyes, and a hawk's nose. There was an intriguing, crescent-shaped scar off the right corner of his well-cut mouth. A bit swarthy, with muscular legs, he was two inches taller than Tammy. She thought he looked like a pirate.

Jay turned out to be the love of her life for the next five and a half years. When they met, he was sketching and Tammy was reading Arthur Clarke's *Childhood's End*. He asked her if she was reading science fiction for fun. She told him it was homework, and invited him to come along to the class.

The course which brought them together was called Science and Fiction, and it was full of fascinating ideas. The students watched films and read such books as Frank Herbert's *Dune Chronicles* and *Inter-Ice Age 4* by Kobo Abe. Then they discussed the scientific implications of the works, and the current state of technology.

Jay shared Tammy's love of science fiction, and they read books, went to movies, listened to music, and talked about science, politics, and the future of the world. Jay remade Tammy's world. When she came to college, she was a clean-cut girl from western Pennsylvania. Within a year, she was a bandana-wearing hippie chick. With Jay, Tammy went to her first rock concert and tried Middle Eastern food. She gained weight and grew her thick, strawberry-blonde hair long, all the way to her waist. As for her eyeglasses, the thick black frames of her teen years were replaced by tortoiseshell frames and wire rims.

While Jay, who was very smart, coasted through his classes, Tammy found college a good deal tougher than high school. She had to work much harder for her grades. She also held a series of work-study jobs to meet expenses. During her first semester she worked as a tutor for the West Philadelphia Free School. Later she was a student social worker at juvenile court. In the summers, she lived off-campus and had jobs as a psychiatric research assistant and worked with the registrar, which kept track of students records.

During her sophomore year, Tammy's mother brought her sisters to Philadelphia and moved them into a rough neighborhood. Tammy felt very depressed. During that year's winter break, to take her mind off her family problems, she volunteered to help out at the Penn Women's Center. For a while she stuffed envelopes, then she began writing satires and literary criticism for the newsletter. When they needed someone to teach a course on the history of witchcraft at the Free Women's University, Tammy took the job. It paid $75.

Tammy had been interested in witchcraft since middle school, when she had made a love potion for one of her school friends. The potion did not work, but she kept reading about the subject and found that it came up a lot in mythology. Tammy divided the college course into different eras of magical study and belief. It included the classical world, cults of the Mother Goddess, the Inquisition, the

Salem witch trials, and modern-day practices like Voodoo and Wicca.

Tammy's research into witchcraft served her well as a writer. Many of her leading characters are healers and mages who use magical spells. When she came to write her own books, rather than making things up, she was careful to use real but benign material as the foundation for her magical scenes. She referred to trusted sources, including a series of books by Scott Cunningham on stones and crystals, herbs and plants, the elements, and other topics, based on Wiccan, Native American, and other religious practices.

Tammy enjoyed most of her psychology courses. She also took two film courses that were both interesting and valuable in her later work. One course put films into their historical setting—the time in which they were made—and the other taught her how to dissect movies shot by shot and angle by angle.

By junior year, Jay had transferred to a college near his home in upstate New York, and Tammy only saw him on weekends. She moved to a house on Pine Street with her friend Ruth Anderson, a tall, Swedish blonde, and some male housemates. It was Ruth who first introduced Tammy to the world of martial arts films. Ruth took Tammy to see a Bruce Lee film, *Enter the Dragon*, and when Tammy saw the delicate Chinese maiden, played by Angela Mao, kick the stuffing out of the bad guys, she was hooked.

Tammy had always been fascinated by fight scenes in films. From the time she was small, she watched them very closely to impress on her mind the different sword moves and fist fights. She picked apart the scenes to decide if they were believable. Then she tried to write about them.

Now, she watched Bruce Lee and other martial artists' films over and over. She analyzed the karate and kung fu

While at college, Tamora Pierce accompanied a friend to see the Bruce Lee film, Enter the Dragon. *Bruce Lee (pictured here in a scene from* Enter the Dragon *in 1973) was a martial arts expert, whose films began a martial arts craze in the 1970s. Tammy became a real fan of Lee's action films, and soon began reading and writing about the martial arts.*

fight scenes in the same way, picking them apart to see if the moves seemed real. She bought books and talked to martial artists whenever she could find them. They even showed her a few moves she could try out for herself. All that she was learning would someday be used in her books.

Other battles in Tammy's life were all too real. Since she had left home, her sister Kim had been having a lot of trouble with their mother. Within a month of moving to Philadelphia, Kim took off and went to live in a group home. Melanie stuck it out for six months, and then she also left, staying with friends or sleeping on Tammy's couch when she could.

Finally, Melanie tracked down their father, Wayne. He had married Mary Lou not long after his divorce with Jackie was final. He invited Melanie to come and live with them in California. But she found that she did not like their rules and came back after a couple of weeks.

One day, while staying with Tammy, Melanie went to visit her mother. She came back badly bruised and bleeding, and said their mother had thrown her against the refrigerator. Tammy took her to the emergency room. The doctor told her that he was going to take pictures of Melanie's injuries and send them to social services because she had been abused.

Tammy was shocked. She had been taking social work courses at college, but she had never put two and two together. A year earlier, at the group home, Kim had alleged her mother had abused her, but when the adults asked Tammy about it, she had said no. As far as she knew, that was just the way her family acted, it was not abuse. Now, after talking to the doctor, Tammy called Kim's group home and told them she had been wrong. She had not understood that what was going on in their house was the same thing she was reading about in class.

Their father applied for custody of Kim, and Tammy

testified at a court hearing. He and Mary Lou were moving to Buhl, Idaho, and they took Kim with them, giving her a normal life for her high school years. Melanie preferred the group home setting, and found a good one. Tammy visited her and went to her school plays.

Tammy would not see her mother again for eight years. A few months earlier, Jackie had thrown Tammy out of her house for being unsympathetic. Tammy decided this time she was going to stay thrown out. She was tired of the emotional whipsawing, being pulled about in two opposite ways at once. She applied for independent status at the university so she no longer had to rely on her mother to sign her financial papers. A year later, Tammy would look back and wonder if the act of establishing her independence from her mother freed her mind enough to start writing again.

One day, at the house on Pine Street, Tammy, Jay, Ruth, and their housemate Niles decided to hop into a Volkswagen Beetle and drive down to Florida to watch the space mission launch. Their trip never got off the ground, but something more important did.

The boys both had long hair, and Tammy had flashes of what might happen driving through the Deep South. All of sudden, there was a story in her head. She sat down at a typewriter and, word by word, the story came out, all five pages of it. It was about a cop in the Deep South who pulls over some apparent hippies in a beat-up Volkswagen Beetle and finds he has come across a couple of demons. She called the story "Demon Chariot." It was the first complete short story she had written in five years. She had blasted through her writer's block at last.

Tammy began to write again. One of her stories was a parody of the "confessions" magazine style. These magazines,

Did you know...

Most writers have a routine that helps them maintain the discipline of writing, such as working at a particular time each day. After business correspondence, errands, and appointments, Tamora Pierce sits down to write around 3 P.M.

She begins by reading and editing the pages she wrote the day before to get her ready for the day's writing. Rather than write a set number of hours per day, she writes a set number of pages. She cannot watch television until she has met her goal. No matter how many pages she has set for herself, she usually manages to complete them before 8 or 9 P.M.

Tammy starts by writing seven pages per day. As the deadline approaches, she increases it to 14–15 pages or more. She limits her breaks to 20 minutes before returning to the desk to write at least two pages before she gets up again.

When she nears the end of a book she will print it out and go over it by hand. "You catch things on the printed page that you won't on the computer screen," she says.* If there is time, she also reads it aloud, for the same reason.

After making any corrections, she has her first draft. Later, she will incorporate the editor's suggestions into a second draft. Usually, just two drafts per book is all she needs. If it is the first book of a series, it might take three drafts to set up new characters and a new setting for the story.

* Donna Dailey's interviews with Tamora Pierce, May–July 2005.

popular in the 1940s–1970s, featured morality tales written in the first person. Tammy's girlfriends enjoyed her story, so she thought she had nothing to lose by sending it out. The third magazine she tried, *Intimate Story*, bought it. In May 1975, she received a letter and a check for $75. Tammy was over the moon. She had made her first sale.

Later she wrote and sold another one, but after that she stopped because she was tired of the confessions formula. It was a bit sickly, like an overripe tropical fruit. "I was always grateful to them for giving me such immediate reinforcement," Tammy said. "There's nothing like a check to tell you that you're doing something right."[19]

Selling a story gave her the courage to take a writing class in short fiction in her senior year. She still felt very shaky. She did not know if she was any good, and she was not finishing a lot of stories. Only 14 students were accepted into the course and it was tough to get in. She did not tell anyone she had sold a story when she began the class. She just felt grateful to be there.

At first, the class did not go well. The teacher was cold and seemed threatened by her students. Then she developed medical problems, and a new teacher took over. His name was David Bradley, and he had just published his first novel, *South Street*. He had a wild mane of hair flowing from beneath a bald crown, a wild beard and was dressed very smartly. To Tammy, it was like a storm had entered the room.

Once again, she had found a valuable mentor. It was not so much that he taught her any great secrets of writing, but he did give her confidence. Stories were read out loud anonymously in class and the other students critiqued them. Tammy was the only person writing speculative fiction (that is, fantasy and science fiction). One day they ripped her story to shreds. She was devastated.

After class, she went up to Bradley and asked him timidly, "Was it that bad?" He looked at her as if she had lost her mind and replied, "No, it was that good."[20]

That incident alone taught her a great deal. Later, during their teacher conference, she found out that Bradley was also from southwestern Pennsylvania. He asked her about her life, and after they had talked a while he told her she should be writing a novel. She laughed in his face, because only a year before she had not been writing at all.

Bradley thought she should write about her experiences when she was growing up. She did try, but after six pages, the writing dried up, and she could see the dread specter of another five years of writer's block. Although she wanted to please him, she thought, maybe it does not matter so much what my first novel is about, maybe the thing that matters is to finish one.

"When you've been writing around 20- or 30-page stories, as I had, that wall between a short story and a novel seems insurmountable," Tammy said. "I thought, maybe what matters is just breaking through that wall."[21]

She thought back to a time when her writing was like breathing, when the words just spilled out and it was all she could do to keep up. At that time she had been in middle school, writing fantasy stories about girl warriors. She decided to try that.

Tammy hammered away on a tale about a girl who disguised herself as a male knight in order to win a tournament and become prime minister. She finished it in June 1976. It was only 112 pages, but it was a book-length manuscript.

"It was rancid, " she said, "a major piece of gorgonzola."[22] She never showed it to anyone. She put it away and went back to writing short stories. It was not even worth rewriting. But it had done what she needed it to do. She had broken through the wall.

In 1976, inspired by a dream, Tamora Pierce (center) began writing her own version of a female heroine based on her younger sister Kim Pierce (left). In 1977 she finished writing her novel entitled The Song of the Lioness, and in 1978 she moved to Buhl, Idaho, to live with her father, Wayne Pierce (right), and stepmother Mary Lou. It was in Buhl, working at the McAuley Home for Girls that she found she could direct The Song of the Lioness to a young adult reading audience. Although she did not know it at the time, Tammy was on her way to finding her favorite audience.

Starting Out

TAMMY WAS MEANT TO GRADUATE in June 1976. But in order to receive her degree in psychology, she had to complete two courses in statistics. Math was her worst subject, and she flunked the second course twice. However, what mattered to her now was that she was writing again.

That summer she took her second writing course, Writing for Television and Film, at Temple University. After class, she would go to the $1 matinee at the cinema and watch Bruce Lee in *Return of the Dragon*. Then she would go home and write.

Tammy got an A in her writing course, and in August she applied for an individual degree in Human Studies. She used all of her credits in social work, education, psychiatry, psychology, and philosophy to persuade the University of Pennsylvania that she deserved it, and at last she received her Bachelor of Arts degree.

Tammy moved to Kingston, in upstate New York, to be with Jay. They lived in a van for awhile. Tammy found the bohemian life tough. Jay's mother disliked Tammy, and blamed her for Jay's failure to finish college. Eventually they got an apartment. But they were already starting to grow apart.

Jay wanted a party girl. He felt that he had not signed on for a writer. Tammy, however, saw no value in frittering her time away. She was determined to write. Once they were settled in the apartment, she told Jay she had to write 10 pages a day, and he went off to the parties without her.

In November, Tammy had a powerful dream. Although she did not remember many details when she woke up, an image stayed in her mind. It was the inspiration for her next book. She sat down and typed up the first scene. Then she wrote the next scene, and the next. She discussed ideas for the story with Jay as they were driving around, and jotted them down in a notebook.

She kept writing 10 pages a day, typing them out on manila paper with Jay's typewriter. Most of the time, the story seemed to spill out of her. In March 1977, she finished a book-length manuscript about a girl who wanted to become a knight. Jay came up with the title: *The Song of the Lioness*.

Tammy turned people she knew from her childhood and teenage years into characters in the book. *The Song of the Lioness*'s heroine, Alanna, was based on her sister Kim. Jay's friends were all drafted into the story, although they did not know it. Her eighth grade math teacher became Duke Gareth. Her friend Warren Knisbaum was Gary. And the model for Duke Roger—the character who is killed twice—was her handsome, but obsessive, high-school boyfriend Chris Henderson.

Tammy knew she had to rewrite the book before sending it out. Revision was nowhere near as fun as the writing had been, and it took her a lot longer. But it was not getting anywhere sitting in a pile on her desk.

By then, she and Jay had started to dissolve their relationship. Tammy got a job with the Kingston Tax Assessment Office. That fall, she took her cat, Fido, and moved into an apartment of her own. She and Jay broke up for good in January.

Tammy kept writing. She sold an article about a local tax revolt, and started sending *The Song of the Lioness* out to publishers.

In August 1978, Wayne and Tammy's stepmother Mary Lou, whom she called "Ma," invited Tammy to come and live with them in Idaho. She thought it would be nice to renew her ties with her father, and she wanted to see Kim again. So she packed up Fido and her belongings and moved to Buhl.

There, she was hired as a house mother at a group home, the McAuley Home for Girls. It was the only time she would ever have a job doing something she had trained to do in college.

Tammy liked the job a lot. She worked full time, one week on, and one week off. On average there were six girls there at any time. The youngest was 14 years old. About half had criminal records, the rest were either neglected, or were constant runaways. Two of the girls already had children of their own.

It was a very strict home, and the girls were not allowed off the grounds except for school or when under staff supervision. If they were well behaved, they were allowed to go out one night a week. They also had an allowance and could go shopping once a week.

Twenty years later, Tammy wrote and sold a short story based on her first week working at the McAuley Home for Girls. The girls had put her through the wringer, testing to see how she would hold up. They needed a lot of attention and got into a lot of mischief. It was hard work, and sometimes they drove her crazy, but overall she liked the girls, and she liked the other staff she worked with.

The girls wanted to read *The Song of the Lioness*, even though it was not yet published, but the director said no. Tammy had written it as an adult novel, and he felt that it contained material that was inappropriate for them. So Tammy told them the story instead, editing it as she went for the teenagers. The girls loved it and got caught up in Alanna's adventures. Every day after school or before bedtime, they would drag her to the dining room saying "Tell us more about Alanna." With the manuscript in her lap, Tammy would continue the story.

In her time off, Tammy wrote a long, science fiction saga with the girls as characters and herself as their fictional house mother, Dr. Pierce, taking them on adventures through space where they got to meet their favorite rock stars and actors. The girls looked forward to each new chapter, which Tammy read to them when she came back on duty. She also wrote a Christmas story for them and gave them all copies. They really enjoyed it, and Tammy was especially pleased when they tried writing themselves.

When she was not at the group home, Tammy lived with her parents for the first six months. Later, she shared an

Did you know...

Tamora Pierce based her famous heroine, Alanna the Lioness, on her sister, Kimberly. Tammy recalled:

> Kim's first word was "No," and I knew she meant it because her teeth were buried in my finger at the time. In a family of mule-headed hillbillies, my sister was regarded as an artist at being stubborn. She was the most obstinate kid I ever knew. I found out from that first bite that it was really difficult to get Kim to let go.

When she created Alanna, Tammy figured that was the kind of personality she would need to disguise herself as a boy for eight years and study the arts of combat. "If she wanted something that badly, Kim would be that determined," she said. "Later, when it begins to bother Alanna that she lies to people she respects and cares about, I knew that would be something that would bother Kim, too."

Like Alanna, Kim always spoke her mind and had a terrifying strength of will. Tammy said:

> Even when we were locked in battle over a toy or a book, I admired her so much. She was ferociously intelligent, and always got good grades.

After serving in the Air Force, Kim earned two bachelors and two masters degrees. She now lives in South Dakota with her husband, and works in a hospital as a flight paramedic and ER nurse. "She saves lives every day," Tammy said. "She really is a hero."

Quoted material from Donna Dailey's interviews with Tamora Pierce, May–July 2005.

apartment with the other house mothers. Tammy liked Mary Lou a great deal. She was glad to see her father happy. Wayne and Mary Lou were like two peas in a pod: hard-working, thrifty, solid blue-collar people. They liked camping and motorcycles. They formed the Idaho Motorcycle Club, which held functions to raise money for charity.

Tammy's father was, as ever, rough around the edges. He refused to talk about Jackie, saying, "no," "it's over," and "forget all that."[23] But one night, he became upset while watching a television movie about an abused wife. He shot out of his seat and stomped out of the room, saying, "Why don't they ever talk about the woman abusing the husband?"[24] At last Tammy realized the truth about her parents' violent marriage, and it was as if a light had been shone on the past.

Their reunion in Idaho was not trouble free. Tammy clashed with Wayne and Mary Lou because they thought she was impractical. She was not frugal like they were. They tried to put her on a budget, which caused a lot of friction. Tammy made a small salary at the group home, and she had debts from college and credit card bills. Her parents were upset when she spent money on books she could not really afford. And they felt if she was not going to write things that sold she should give up the fantasy stories, get her life together, and get a real job. Tammy respected them and understood where they were coming from, but their way of living was not hers.

Wayne and Mary Lou also could not understand why she cared so much about the kids in the group home. She told them that she and her sisters could so easily have ended up in trouble themselves. Two days before Thanksgiving, Mary Lou came in with two bags of groceries and said, "These are

In 1979, Tamora Pierce left the McAuley Home for Girls where she had worked for a year, and moved to New York City to launch her writing career. Tammy loved the city and she pursued her passion for martial arts by writing a martial arts movie script and taking karate lessons. In this 1980 picture, Tammy relaxes from her hectic writing and working schedule.

for your girls."[25] Tammy learned that she could not judge her parents by their words, but by their deeds.

Even when she was arguing with them, Tammy was proud that they were her parents. "I often wished, even though I know I would have turned out very differently, that Mary Lou had been my mother," Tammy said, "because I don't think our family would have busted up with her in charge."[26]

Chris Henderson, Tammy's boyfriend from high school, came to visit. He was also writing, and told her that if she wanted to get her writing career going, she needed to go to New York City. By now, Tammy had been in Idaho for one year. She was feeling burnt out on her job, and had clashed with the director of the group home, who did not appreciate anyone questioning his way of handling the home. She could see that she was getting on her parents' nerves, and her poor sister, Kim, was caught in the middle.

A move to New York seemed like a good idea. Although she was sorry to leave the girls, she quit her job and headed back east by bus in early August 1979.

When she arrived in New York City, Chris said she could sleep on his couch. That lasted all of two weeks. He proceeded to cut *The Song of the Lioness* down, saying that the book was immature. Tammy felt like she had in the writing class, only this time she knew what was behind it. Chris felt threatened by her work and was trying to make her feel bad about it. Nonetheless, she felt her writing begin to wither.

Chris introduced her to his soon-to-be ex-wife, PJ, and PJ's friend, Bobby. When Tammy met PJ for lunch, PJ noticed that Tammy was upset and asked why. Tammy told her that Chris was making her crazy and she did not know what to do about it. "Easy," PJ replied, "you're going to come and live with us."[27]

Soon Tammy found herself living in the heart of midtown Manhattan. The apartment building was on 8th Avenue between 54th and 55th streets, on the outermost edges of Times Square. She was four blocks from Central Park, and close to the theater district and Carnegie Hall—right in the middle of everything.

"It was Dream City," Tammy remembered. "It helped if you had money, but it was still a very cool place to be, especially if you were young and weren't bothered if you didn't have all the mod cons [modern conveniences]."[28]

Tammy and Bobby shared a studio apartment with a bathroom down the hall. There was no closet and they put their clothes on a step ladder. PJ moved in with Lynn, an artist, across the hall. Also on their floor were a karate school, an actors' studio, a ballet studio, and a disco dance and skate studio.

Tammy felt like she was in a movie about artists in New York. Bobby, who was gay, worked in a thrift shop while trying to set up a jewelry business. PJ was writing articles, Lynn was painting, and Tammy was writing. They would sit in the hall and work, and the actors, dancers, skaters, and martial arts students would come and hang out with them.

Just talking with everyone was very valuable for Tammy. She learned that they were all dealing with the same issues in creativity; it was just the final expression that was different.

Tammy soaked up martial arts whenever she could. She watched competitions, live or on television. She learned which moves were solid techniques, and which were mere show moves, sometimes done with wires. The movie theaters on 42nd Street were cheap at the time, and she could afford to go to the movies often. She wrote film reviews for martial arts magazines. She wrote and directed a student martial arts movie, shot by her friend Andy. She also met up with her old friend from California, Mike Dilts, who had a bit part in the film.

Tammy began taking martial arts lessons at the karate school, or *dojo*, down the hall. It was small and friendly, and she liked it. But after a year, she tore a muscle taking her yellow belt test and had to take time off. Before she could resume her lessons, her teacher closed the *dojo* and went off to Southeast Asia to train as a *kendo* swordsman.

To support herself, Tammy worked as a temporary secretary. She also applied to agencies that dealt with jobs in the publishing industry. One of them would lead her to the break she had been hoping for.

In addition to her full-time job, Tamora Pierce read manuscripts for Silhouette Romances and continued to write daily. Although Tammy struggled to find a publisher for her books, she finally found an editor. Here we see Tammy in her very first author publicity photo.

Radio Days

ON OCTOBER 31, 1979, TAMMY started a new, full-time job at the Harold Ober literary agency. She thought she was in literary heaven. The founder of the agency had been F. Scott Fitzgerald's agent, and the office was lined with books by the many famous writers they represented, including William Faulkner, Agatha Christie, J.D. Salinger, and Judy Blume. It was like walking into a temple of literature.

Tammy was the office assistant for all of the agents there. She did a little bit of everything: filing and paperwork, typing up rights and permissions, fees and copyright notices for Ober properties, and sending out royalty statements.

In addition to this full-time job, Tammy was also reading unsolicited manuscripts for Silhouette Romances, a popular publisher of romance novels. Unsolicited manuscripts are works submitted by unknown authors in the hopes that they will be published. Tammy's job was to read the manuscript, write a summary of the plot, and give her opinion of it. She recommended whether a manuscript should receive further consideration or be returned with a polite rejection note. It was a very educational process for a would-be author.

Meanwhile, Tammy wrote some literary short stories that took place in the real world. She had also written a martial arts novel. But they did not sell. *The Song of the Lioness* had received four rejection slips, so when she started at the literary agency, her novel was on hold while she thought about her options for polishing it up.

Tammy sat next to Craig Tenney, then the chief office assistant. Craig taught her the ropes at the agency. When he found out she had a book making the rounds, Craig told another colleague, Frances Langer, who told Tammy to show the manuscript to one of their agents, Claire Smith. At first, Tammy was afraid they might fire her for conflict of interest. She did not know that publishing is filled with people who write, hoping to get their foot in the door. Frances would not leave her alone until she showed *The Song of the Lioness* to Claire.

Finally, around March, she worked up the courage to tell Claire about her novel. The agent simply said, "I'll read it." About a week later, she handed it back and told Tammy she should rewrite it as four books for teenagers.

Since Claire had only read half the book, Tammy did not take her seriously. She was surprised a few months later when Claire asked her how the rewrites were coming along.

Tammy replied that she had thought she was just being nice. Claire looked at her with one eyebrow raised and her mouth curled to one side. "Tammy," she said, "I am never nice."[29] Tammy had worked in publishing long enough by then to know that agents cannot afford to encourage people unless they really feel their writing might have a chance to be published.

Because she had told the story to her girls at the group home, editing it for teenagers as she spoke, Tammy knew she could do it. On evenings and weekends she sat down and started to rewrite her 732-page novel into a quartet of four separate books telling the story of Alanna of Trebond, a girl who wants to become a knight in the kingdom of Tortall.

In Tortall, girls are not allowed to become warriors, so Alanna comes up with the plan to changes places with her twin brother, Thom. Thom was supposed to go train to become a knight, but he wanted to become a mage (or magic-worker). Together they revise the letters their father had written to read that he has twin sons rather than a son and a daughter. The story continues, telling of how Alanna, disguised as a boy for eight years, struggles to master combat weapons, magic, and herself, making powerful friends and enemies as she rises to become a legend in her time.

One Sunday night in 1981, a friend dragged Tammy away from her writing to go to Bogie's Restaurant, where a group of people met each week to listen to old mystery radio plays. They called their informal group the Friends of Bogie's, because of the restaurant they met at and as a tribute to Humphrey Bogart. Some of the mystery fans decided to record an old radio play for themselves. Tammy played several parts, and they recorded it on a little cassette recorder. As she read the script, she thought, "I could do this."[30]

In her spare time she wrote a play script. Because there

were more women in the group than men, she made the hero go up against an all-female criminal gang. The mystery fans loved it. They put out a casting call, and upgraded their equipment. As the year progressed, in addition to working at the agency and rewriting *The Song of the Lioness*, Tammy also helped start an amateur radio company that performed original, new radio comedy and drama.

In October, Tammy finished the rewrite for *Alanna: The First Adventure*. Claire Smith became her first agent and began proposing the book to various publishing houses. The first two publishers turned it down. Then Claire sent it to Jean Karl at Atheneum Books. Jean sent back a three-page letter saying "no," but Claire saw something in that three-page reply, and asked Jean if she would meet with the author to talk about rewrites. Jean agreed.

Tammy did not see the point, but she knew Claire was a good agent and she knew enough to listen to her. What she did not know at the time was that Jean Karl was a legend in children's publishing. She edited some of the top children's authors, and her name on a book would guarantee a sale to any knowledgeable booksellers and librarians.

At their meeting, Jean was very quiet as Tammy explained how the book had begun as a single novel, and that she knew exactly where the next three books were going to go and what would happen to Alanna in them. They also talked about a science fiction novel and other ideas Tammy had in mind. Jean told her what she thought the books needed in order to be successful.

When the hour was up, they shook hands and Jean told Tammy she would take the series if Tammy made the changes they had discussed. Tammy thanked her very politely, then thanked Jean's secretary very politely, and left the office. It was not until she was punching the button for the elevator that she realized she had just sold her first book.

When she signed the contract, Tammy called her parents in Idaho to share the news. Mary Lou just said "Well that's good, I'm glad to hear it, I'll let your father know."[31] Tammy had expected more enthusiasm, and felt disappointed as she hung up the phone. But the next day, a bouquet of flowers arrived and she knew they were proud of her.

"That meant the world to me," she said. "They knew I had something real then. Getting them to be proud of me was something that money couldn't buy."[32]

Meanwhile, the radio company was growing as they brought in more actors and writers. Tammy wrote most of the first season's radio dramas. It became her pattern for the next few years. She would alternate between writing books and writing radio plays. As soon as she finished a book draft, she would go straight into writing a radio play. The plays were very different from her books, usually on contemporary horror or historical themes. It was her brain's way of taking a vacation from Tortall.

Tammy was still working at the literary agency during the day, fitting writing in at night and on the weekends. Between her job and the books and the radio company, it was a busy time. "It's amazing I found any time to think," she said, looking back.[33]

By the spring of 1982, Tammy suggested the Friends of Bogie's form a professional radio company. She thought everyone involved had enough talent, technically as well as in writing and acting, to sell productions. They called the company ZPPR (pronounced "zipper") after the core founders: George Zarr, a musician and songwriter; Tamora Pierce, the scriptwriter; Pam Peterson, who did the sound effects; and their publicist, Denise Robert. Tammy dedicated her second novel, *In the Hand of the Goddess*, to her colleagues with the pun: "Together, we'll go very fast and very far on little tracks."[34]

Tammy made many friends in the company. One of the actors, Raquel Starace, kept mentioning a friend she knew from acting school, Tim Liebe, who she thought would do well in the group. Tammy finally met Tim that August, at Raquel's birthday party. He was 5 foot 10, with fine brownish-blonde hair, sapphire blue eyes, and a very warm smile.

George Zarr's wife, Candy, loved to play matchmaker, and a week later she set Tammy and Tim up on a date. As Tim later put it, the date simply never ended.

Tim, who was two years younger than Tammy, had moved to New York from California to pursue an acting career. Tammy discovered he was highly intelligent, funny, and talented. They both loved movies and reading. Along with acting, Tim was making industrial videos and student films. He was also a good writer. He joined the radio company as both a writer and a director. Tammy was the first at ZPPR to read the material he wrote. Later she encouraged him to write articles for a video magazine, which developed into a second career as a consumer electronics writer.

Where Tammy tended to be rather intense, Tim taught her how to play and be silly. Once, on a bus, he made her laugh so hard she fell off the seat into the aisle. He was very affectionate, even in public.

Tammy had recently moved to an apartment in New Jersey in her friend Pam's house. Tim had a bachelor apartment in a residential hotel in the city. During the week she stayed with him in the city, going home to write on the weekends. This became their routine for a long time.

Alanna: The First Adventure came out in September 1983. The radio company threw a party to celebrate its publication.

Once she signed a contract for the Song of the Lioness quartet, Tamora Pierce was on her way to becoming a successful author. Here Tammy is making her first appearance as a published author at the Books of Wonder bookstore in New York City.

When Tammy received her first hardcover copies, she immediately went from bookstore to bookstore, looking for it. But it was not there. Then, at a B. Dalton bookstore on 8th Street and 6th Avenue, she saw two copies of her book in the children's section. Tim found her there in tears, saying over and over again, "It's real. I can't believe it's real!"[35]

Not long afterwards, Tammy received her first invitation

to an event for authors at Books of Wonder, a bookshop then located on Hudson Street. ZPPR was moving into new premises nearby, and she had spent the day cleaning, painting, and caulking windows with her friends. On the way home, they stopped by the bookstore out of curiosity. Books of Wonder had five copies of *Alanna: The First Adventure*, and her friends made a beeline for them. As they were looking at Tammy's book, one of the booksellers came over and told them, "We can't recommend this book highly enough, especially to parents with girls." Her friends turned to Tammy and said in chorus "She's the author!"[36]

Dressed in cut-off shorts, a T-shirt, and a bandana, Tammy met the proprietors in all her paint-splattered glory. It was the first time she was recognized for her work, and it was extremely gratifying to meet people who loved her writing. The staff at Books of Wonder "raised her up properly,"[37] teaching her how to go into stores and sign her books.

To have her book in the stores was an exciting thing. Tammy did not expect much more than that. She had worked at the agency long enough to know that most authors did not pay back their advance (money paid to an author before publication), and unless they were really lucky, did not go on to a second printing. But a year later, the book was reprinted and Tammy began to earn royalties. "You could have knocked me over with a feather," she said. "I felt grateful and happy."[38]

By now the sequel to the first Song of the Lioness book, *In the Hand of the Goddess*, was well underway. Tammy was still cutting up and pasting down her original manuscript by hand. When she got her advance for the third book, she used it to buy a computer. It changed the way she wrote. Rewrites became easier, and she became much more relaxed about making changes.

The original manuscript for *The Song of the Lioness* no longer exists. Tammy never made a copy of it before she had to cut and paste the original 732-page novel into the four rewrites. But she insists the quartet is much better written than the original novel because she learned so much in the process of revision.

Invariably, when she followed Jean Karl's advice, the books got better. Tammy said:

> I realized what a master editor can do. Jean was the best, and I learned so much from her, how to make it tighter and clearer. I learned from the suggestions in her editorial letters, and from reading the typeset galleys and seeing what changes she'd made to the book.[39]

Usually, after the second draft, Jean would be pleased with Tammy's rewrites. The only time they ever had a tussle was over the first draft for the fourth book, *Lioness Rampant*. Originally in that book, Alanna would drink brandy if she felt faint or was injured. It was historically accurate. Spirits were the preferred restorative in the Middle Ages. But although Jean did not object to the sex and violence in the stories, she felt it was inappropriate to portray the use of alcohol to young readers. Tammy finally came up with a compromise: the brandy was replaced by Liam's herbal concoctions with a smell that would wake the dead. It was the only time they debated any controversial subjects in Tammy's books.

Jean was Tammy's editor for her first eight books, the Song of the Lioness quartet and The Immortals quartet which followed.

In 1983, Tammy left her job at the literary agency. Although she liked it, it took up a lot of the time and energy she needed for writing. She was still working with ZPPR, but it was not earning any money and they were forced to finance their own productions. When her savings ran out, she took up temporary secretarial work to make ends meet.

That year, Tammy saw her mother for the last time. Jackie

Did you know...

There are writers who can make characters up. I'm not one of them. It helps me to have a real person in mind when developing my characters. Most of the time I need to know how they look, how they move, what they sound like. It gives me a leg up and makes it easier to start with someone I know. The characters always grow away from whoever I base them on. In recent years I've found I can also develop characters if I have the right photograph and the right name to work from.*

Tamora Pierce has a large file drawer of photos, broken up by age, gender, and ethnic group. It includes family members, friends, fans, film and television actors, and pictures from magazines or the Internet. She often looks through world magazines because of the variety of her settings. She clips out the pictures, and files them for a rainy day. When Tammy needs a new character, she goes through the files to find a photo that suits her. It goes up on a cork board beside her desk and she uses it to cast the character.

*   Donna Dailey's interviews with Tamora Pierce, May–July 2005.

was in the hospital in the early stages of Huntington's Chorea, a neurological disease that causes irreversible brain damage. Jackie barely knew her daughter. Tammy recalled:

> It was like someone had taken a cloth and wiped away all of the cynicism and rage and disappointment from her face and left it as smooth and uncaring and basically cheerful as a baby's. She actually seemed happy, so in a way, the disease did her a bit of a favor there.[40]

But the mother Tammy had known was no longer present. By the end of the decade Jackie was in a vegetative state. She died in 1993 in a state institution.

Over the next few years, Tammy worked on the Song of the Lioness quartet. *In the Hand of the Goddess* was published in the spring of 1984. Despite the publication of the books, she was still struggling financially.

In 1985, Tammy moved back into the city, to a studio apartment in a residential hotel on 91st Street and Broadway on the Upper West Side. It became her permanent home. She and Tim still kept separate places. Tammy took a job as a secretary at Chase Manhattan bank. It was a perfect arrangement. She had a steady income and health insurance. When the office was not busy, her boss let her write at her desk.

That year, she also sold her first fantasy short story, called "Plain Magic." It appeared in a collection called *Planetfall*, published by Oxford University Press in England.

Her third Song of the Lioness book, *The Woman Who Rides Like a Man*, came out in spring 1986. *Lioness Rampant* was published in fall 1988, completing the series.

In 1985, Tamora Pierce married long-time boyfriend Tim Liebe in a small ceremony in New York. Her "spouse creature," as she calls him, is a writer and a director, so he easily encourages her creativity. Tammy and Tim are seen above at a family reunion in 2000.

A Spouse Creature

ON DECEMBER 14, 1985, around 200 people gathered in a little shadow box theater in Soho, New York. They had come to witness an event they might never have believed had they not seen it with their own eyes: Tammy's and Tim's wedding.

Tammy had always been as reluctant to marry as her heroine Alanna. Tim, too, throughout their long relationship, had insisted he was not interested in marriage. Nonetheless, with the encouragement of their friends, they found themselves before a Unitarian minister the day after Tammy's 31st birthday.

Tammy wore a floor-length, cream kimono with a dusty blue

and rust-colored flower print over a blouse and pants. She had offered to make the supreme sacrifice and wear a dress, but Tim wanted her to be comfortable. He looked splendid in a white dinner jacket. Raquel Starace, who was Tim's best friend, was Best Person. Tammy's bridesmaids wore fire engine red; that color gave her courage, and she needed a lot of it.

Wayne and Mary Lou came into the city from Idaho, but her sister Kim was now in the Air Force and was unable to get leave. Tim's mother, brother, and grandmother came from California. When the tape recorder for the music failed to work, Tim directed everybody to hum Tammy down the aisle. Afterwards, the radio company threw a wedding reception. The couple even got to spend a night at the Algonquin Hotel, a famous New York literary landmark, as a gift from the company. Tammy's father danced with her, and then he danced with Tim. It was a great, fun day.

After the wedding, Tammy and Tim shocked their friends by keeping Tim's bachelor apartment, where he continued to go on weekends. Tammy explained:

> The one thing we agreed upon when we got married was that if it wasn't broke, we didn't want to fix it. When we were first going together, we realized that we each needed a lot of time for our creative lives, as well as the life we had together. We don't live in each other's laps all the time. We allow each other a lot of space. I think that's one reason we have lasted together.[41]

They were able to keep things the way they were for about five years, until finances got too tight and they had to give up the second apartment. Because Tim was also a writer, actor, and aspiring film-maker, he understood that part of Tammy would always be focused on her work.

Her career never threatened him, he was never jealous. He loves Tammy's books, and her beloved "spouse creature" has become an important helpmate in her creative process.

Over the years they have talked about the characters as if they were people they knew: who's doing what, who's having babies, what's going on in the kingdoms. Tim often remembers more about them than Tammy herself. When Tammy gets stuck with a storyline or has a new idea to work through, he is the first person she goes to and they bat ideas back and forth. Tammy said:

> There are hundreds of plot solutions in the books that are Tim's suggestion. In the Daine books, making the Stormwings less monstrous and more human was his idea. The fact that Lord Wyldon in the Kel books is not an out-and-out bad guy but a more complicated person was all Tim's idea, too.[42]

If there are long lines at Tammy's book signings, Tim will often talk to the fans and parents and answer questions while they wait. For years, he has helped her and author Meg Cabot run the Sheroes website—a discussion forum where people can talk about female heroes.

In 1987, Tammy left Chase Manhattan and moved with her boss to a new job at Prudential-Bache Capital Funding. But the corporate atmosphere and pressure there left her far too drained to write when she got home at night. She quit in April 1988, and returned to her old job at Chase Manhattan.

That same year, Tammy also left ZPPR. She disagreed with the direction it was taking and was tired of the political maneuvering. This move freed up more time for her writing.

Soon Tammy realized she needed to get out of permanent

work and concentrate on writing. She went back to temporary secretarial work for a legal firm. The office was at the tip of Manhattan, near Castle Clinton, and she used to see the old-timers there feeding sparrows from their hands. She asked them their secret, and they told her it was broken-up peanut bits. She thought it would be cool to get the sparrows to do that for her.

After she was finished writing *Lioness Rampant*, Tammy began a historical mystery in which a young girl goes back in time to samurai Japan. She wrote three chapters and an outline, but when no publisher picked it up, she put it aside.

Tammy decided to return to the world of Tortall to see what was happening in the kingdom 10 years later. While her first heroine, Alanna, had been written for who she wanted to be at the age of 12, her new character, Daine, reflected how Tammy saw herself at around age 30: semi-reclusive, and better at dealing with animals than people.

Many influences from Tammy's own life worked their way into the new series, called The Immortals. It follows the progress of the young orphan Daine, as she discovers and develops her special gift of wild magic, which enables her to talk with, and even become, animals. When the world is invaded by fabled creatures called "immortals," Daine's unique parentage and abilities are the key to saving Tortall.

Once again, Tammy drew on real people as the models for her characters. The actress Trini Alvarado, who played Meg in the 1994 film *Little Women*, personified Tammy's mental image of Daine, which had initially been inspired by a picture of a girl on a card surrounded by a spilled basket of kittens, some birds, and a lizard. (By pure coincidence, the actress hired by Listening Library to read the audio versions

When writing a new series, Tamora Pierce's characters are often inspired by real people. The Immortals series is about a young girl named Daine, who Tammy modeled after actress Trini Alvardo. Alvardo is seen here in her role as Meg in the film **Little Women.**

of the Song of the Lioness and the Trickster books is none other than Trini Alvarado.)

With his distinctive voice, height, and youthful personality, the actor Jeff Goldblum struck the right image for the mage Numair, who becomes Daine's teacher, friend, and later her lover.

Tammy lived near Riverside Park in New York, and she started going there to observe the wildlife in the city. She brought books to identify the birds she saw, and took broken-up peanuts to hand feed the sparrows. She did not get a nibble from them for years, but the squirrels were never shy.

Did you know...

Tamora Pierce's many years of reading mythology paid off when writing The Immortals quartet. The gods and goddesses in her books are based on those found in world myths and legends. Daine's father Weiryn, for example, a minor god of the hunt, is based on the Celtic god, Herne the Hunter, while the Graveyard Hag is a classic Crone figure.

So, too, are the terrifying immortal creatures that invade Tortall. The Stormwings and Coldfangs were initially based, respectively, on the harpies and furies from Greek mythology. But Tammy objected to the fact they were all female. Her Stormwings are a marriage of metal and flesh, foul-smelling, half-bird, half-human creatures that desecrate the bodies of the dead on battlefields.

For the Coldfangs, she broke away completely. Recalling a nature program where David Attenborough picked up a sluggish gila monster in the Arizona desert, she made the Coldfangs into giant lizards.

Basilisks, too, originated in mythology, as creatures with a goat's head, a lion's body, and a snake's tail. Tammy decided there was no way something like that could live. So she based the character Tkaa on a basilisk lizard, making him bigger, more colorful, and with more control over his ability to turn things to stone.

For all the immortals, she experimented with their appearance in the Dover Coloring Book of Mythological Creatures. Tammy worked her way through the series in this manner, examining real myths and legends, using some things, and changing others.

They came right up to her, and helped themselves to her peanuts and even her sandwich. Soon she was naming her "regulars"—the first she called Mrs. Wartnose. Feeding the birds and squirrels became a form of meditation and helped her forget about her money worries for awhile. She became more and more interested in the natural world.

Tammy's friend Raquel was a big supporter of conservation programs for wolves and bats. Her interest inspired Tammy, and a wolf pack became a central part of Daine's story. Tammy was also watching nature programs by Sir David Attenborough. She was so enchanted by his adventures and the fact he would pick up any animal, that she made him the basis for the character Lindhall Reed in the third book, *The Emperor Mage*.

All of these things swirled together in the Daine books. When Tammy wrote about Daine's relationship with animals, she described what she wished she could do herself. The squirrel Flicker in *Wolf-Speaker* was based on real squirrels Tammy knew from the park. The sparrows she fed, including Freckle, Crown, and Arrow, appeared later in the Kel books. Even her own cats—nicknamed Blueness and Scrap—had supporting roles in *Wolf-Speaker*.

As Tammy was writing *Wild Magic*, she found she was rapidly losing patience with secretarial work. As long as the work was simple typing, filing, and taking dictation, she was not emotionally engaged with the jobs and she had the energy to work full time and still write at night. She thought if she just pressed harder, maybe she could get more books out and be able to live solely on her writing income.

Wild Magic was published in 1992. By that time Tammy was making more and more money from royalties, especially from German and British sales of her books. This convinced her she could take the risk. Tim was working as a temporary secretary and part-time video editor. He encouraged her to give it a try. Although they would have very lean times for awhile, Tammy took the leap and began writing full time.

While she was working on her next book, *Wolf-Speaker*, some difficulties arose with her publisher, Atheneum. The company was being bought by MacMillan, and they were not sure they were going to be able to publish the last two books in the series. *Wolf-Speaker* was not published until the spring of 1994.

Tammy wrote some of her most vivid and glittering images in *The Emperor Mage*, the third book of The Immortals quartet. In one of his music videos, singer Ozzy Ozbourne was the perfect model of decadence for Emperor Ozorne, dressed in a pearl-studded white tunic with makeup, nail polish, and gold beads in his hair. For the opulent capital of Carthak, Tammy researched Carthage, a Phoenician colony, as well as Assyria, Babylonia, and other ancient kingdoms. In the ancient Egyptian wing of the Metropolitan Museum of Art in New York, she studied the funerary offerings for images of their day-to-day lives, and how their houses and rooms were laid out. A Roman cookbook and a book called *Unmentionable Cuisine* gave her ideas for the lavish banquets.

In the end, the Atheneum did publish the full quartet. *The Emperor Mage* came out in the summer of 1995. The final book, *Realms of the Gods*, was published in the fall of 1996.

Tammy's editor, Jean Karl, had become a freelance editor and she edited The Immortals series from her home. Without Jean in the office to oversee the artwork, covers, jacket copy, and other details, Tammy was not always pleased with the results. Coupled with her frustration over the delay on the last two books, Tammy felt it was time for a change.

Fascinated by everyday magic, Tamora Pierce wanted to write a new series that was different from her usual style. Tammy wrote the Circle of Magic series about a group of heroes rather than a lone heroine and changed the location to the Middle East, where legends and mysticism thrive.

9

Weaving a
Magic Circle

AFTER *REALMS OF THE GODS* was published, Tammy decided to leave Atheneum. Her agent approached Scholastic to see if they would publish the quartet in paperback. They wanted something new, and asked if she had anything else in mind.

Tammy did. She was ready for a break from the world of Tortall. And an idea had been brewing in her head for a long time. When she was living with her parents in Idaho, as they sat in the living room watching television, Mary Lou and Kim had been talking and crocheting, turning balls of yarn into cloth, apparently without paying any attention to it at all. As she watched the needles fly, Tammy thought, "If that isn't magic, I don't know what is."[43]

When she watched people sewing or quilting, blowing glass, working metal, doing carpentry, or growing plants, it all looked like magic to her. She wanted to write a story in which the magic is dependent on things that most people dismiss as ordinary.

Tammy had already mentioned thread magic in some of her earlier tales, such as *The Woman Who Rides Like a Man*. One of her actor friends from the radio company, Thomas Gansevoort, was also an artist who had worked with just about every craft. She knew she could call on him for advice if she got stuck.

For the new series, Tammy thought it would be fun to work with a group hero instead of a lone heroine as she had done in the past. She also wanted to build a new universe from the ground up. She explained:

> I felt the background of white, medieval Europe was the fantasy author's default setting. I wanted to move away from that. The other part of the world I've always been fascinated with is the medieval Middle East and Central Asia at the time of the Silk Road. It was a crossroads, a melting pot. Something of every culture meets there.[44]

Up on her wall, Tammy had a map of the world's "hot spots," which in the mid-1990s included the Middle East, Iraq, and Iran. Looking at it, she realized that between the Caspian Sea, the Persian Gulf, and the Mediterranean Sea, she literally had a crossroads of the world right there. So she took down the map, cut out the seas, turned it over and photocopied it down and fiddled with it until she had a land mass for her new world: Emelan and the Pebbled Sea.

Sadly, Claire Smith, Tammy's agent, became ill with

cancer in the early 1990s and decided to retire. The Harold Ober literary agency wanted to keep representing Tammy, but the company had no other agent who specialized in children's books. After some discussion, her friend at the agency, Craig Tenney, agreed to represent her. He took over as her agent for the new series, The Circle of Magic.

The four heroes in the story—Sandry, Tris, Daja, and Briar—are all, for one reason or another, orphans or outcasts. Rescued by the mage Niklaren Goldeye, they are brought to the temple city of Winding Circle in Summersea. As they discover and learn to master their unique magic gifts, they become inextricably linked through their magic and their friendship.

Tammy's plan was to write two books a year at the 200-page manuscript length. She began work on *Sandry's Book* in 1995. Sandry's magic gift manifests itself through her weaving. As she began her research, Tammy thought she ought to try weaving herself. And to do it right, she should really start with spinning, since spinning wool to thread is the first step. But in her small, one-room apartment, there was no way to make a spinning wheel fit.

Tammy found a catalog from Amazon Pickling and Dry Goods Works, a company based in Davenport, Iowa, which supplied clothing and items from the frontier era through Victorian times. For $50, Tammy bought a kit with a hand (or drop) spindle, wool, and an instructional video that would teach her to spin using a drop spindle. She said:

> I can vouch for every mistake Sandry makes when she's learning to spin, because I made them all. I know every bit as well as she does that wool can unspin itself faster that it took to spin it.[45]

Eventually, after much frustration, she did produce a ball of yarn. And it was a useful thing to do, because in learning to spin, she came up with a metaphor for the whole book. Tammy's spindle is now at Hicklebee's Bookstore in San Jose, California, which displays artifacts that different authors used in their books.

"Dig around in enough little corners, and it's amazing the stuff you turn up," Tammy said.[46] When she came to write *Daja's Book*, she drew on another eclectic source, the Cumberland General Store in Virginia, to find period books on blacksmithing.

In this series, Tammy finally worked up the nerve to create a character based loosely on herself. Tris has Tammy's red hair and spectacles, a plump shape, and a love of storms. Sandry was based on several of Tammy's fans combined. Briar and Daja were Tammy's first two characters to be inspired by striking photographs.

For the children's teachers, Tammy's artist friend Thomas was the model for Niko. Frostpine is the spitting image of Tammy's college mentor, David Bradley, wild hair, bald crown, bushy beard, and all. Lark came from another photograph, while Rosethorn was based on Major Kira Nerys from *Star Trek Deep Space Nine*.

In the books, Tammy drew on her own childhood experiences and those of her sisters and her girls at the group home. In creating Daja's Trader culture, she used a combination of medieval Jews and gypsies, and the treatment they received. For Briar, Tammy remembered the gang members she encountered in Philadelphia. She also drew upon the knowledge that gifted children often end up as outcasts unless they are placed among others like themselves.

"If you are different, one of the things you learn growing up is that life is just not going to be easy—ever," Tammy said. "And you see it in so many different ways."[47]

In The Circle of Magic series, Tammy wanted her characters to face things that kids in our real world face. The four children deal with earthquakes, forest fires, disease, and bandits or pirates. She knew that the best fantasy is thoroughly rooted in reality. When she researched *Briar's Book*, her sister Kim, who had become a paramedic, then a nurse, advised her on epidemic disease.

Sandry's Book was published in the fall of 1997. The others quickly followed. *Tris's Book* and *Daja's Book* came out in 1998, with *Briar's Book* completing the quartet in the spring of 1999.

In the United States, each book in the series was named after one of the four heroes. When they were published in the United Kingdom, however, the titles were changed. *Sandry's Book* became *The Magic in the Weaving*; *Tris's Book* became *The Power in the Storm*; *Daja's Book* became *The Fire in the Forging*; and *Briar's Book* became *The Healing in the Vine*.

Tammy's own magic circle was widening alongside her books. For several years, she had given one or two talks a year at schools and book fairs. In 1995, a group of schools and libraries in the San Francisco Bay area pooled their funds and brought her out on tour. As she made the rounds, talking at different locations, she found herself starting to connect with the kids. She enjoyed the presentations.

When she visits schools, she allows the students to ask her anything they want. She hopes they will then feel comfortable enough to ask her questions about writing and creativity. "That's what I'm there for," she said. "I would have killed to talk to a living writer for five minutes in seventh grade."[48] She began to expand her program of personal appearances. By 2000, Tammy was giving two or three talks a month.

An excited young reader holds Tamora Pierce's new novel, Trickster's Choice, *published in 2003. With* Trickster's Choice, *Tammy proved she could create a variety of characters, although she most enjoys creating tough and capable heroines.*

Tammy also joined Science Fiction and Fantasy Writers of America, a professional organization created to connect people who write science fiction and fantasy. Through this group Tammy met a fellow writer, Michael Burstein, who introduced her to the world of science fiction conventions. When she turned up at Boskone, one of the main conventions held each year in Boston, Massachusetts, over President's Day weekend, she was surprised to find that people recognized her. Soon she was participating in panel discussions and other events, and meeting fantasy and science fiction writers she admired. Now she regularly attends Boskone, Confluence, and other science fiction conventions, as a participant and twice as the guest of honor.

Meanwhile in 1997, Tammy and her agent, Craig Tenney, approached Random House, which had published the paperback editions of The Song of the Lioness quartet, to see if they wanted paperback rights to The Immortals as well. Editor Mallory Loehr was a fan. She grabbed the Daine books, and convinced the company to reissue the Alanna books as well, with brand new covers. Mallory and Tammy hit it off, and she wanted Tammy's input on the covers and artists.

Suddenly, by the end of 1998, Tammy had a massive market presence, with eight paperbacks on the bookstore shelves along with The Circle of Magic quartet. And soon, she would find herself back in the world of Tortall.

Tammy wanted to keep on with the Circle books because she felt she had really gotten involved with the characters. In the next quartet, she wanted to take the young mages four years down the road, when they are dealing with the first students of their own. She also wanted to create a stronger story arc.

In The Circle Opens series, she continued the theme of children dealing with real-world problems by making crime central to the plots of those four books. *Magic Steps* depicts the dangers of drug use when Sandry finds herself involved in a deadly Mafia-type war. Briar comes up against his old street background in *Street Magic*. In *Cold Fire*, Daja confronts a serial arsonist, a story Tammy based on a celebrated case in the United States, while Tris faces a serial killer in

Shatterglass. The books bring a modern sensibility to the crimes which take place in a medieval setting.

The Circle Opens is a darker, more controversial quartet, with a greater number of violent scenes. Tammy felt that since many children and teenagers deal with these issues in their everyday lives, it is good to address them in fiction.

At the same time, Tammy really wanted to write another lady knight story, set in the Tortall universe. Mallory was enthusiastic and agreed to take it on. It set a new pattern for Tammy. From then on, each year she would write one Circle book for Scholastic, and another book for Random House about the kingdom of Tortall.

Tammy already had her heroine in mind. Over the years she had developed pen friendships with some of her readers. One of her fans, called Kelly, was a big, strong girl, about five foot ten inches tall, with broad shoulders and a thick waistline. She was incredibly active and loved hiking, canoeing, and rock-climbing. Tammy recalled:

> People were making her life hell, telling her she should diet, she'd never get a boyfriend, etc., etc. They wanted to turn her into an anorexic stick. I looked at her and saw a gorgeous girl, a beautiful mare. The feeling was borne out when I met my 10-year-old niece, who was already up to my chin and still growing. I wanted to write a book for girls like Kelly and my niece.[49]

Originally, Tammy envisioned the story of Keladry of Mindelan and her quest to become a knight like her hero, Alanna the Lioness, as a trilogy: *Page*, *Squire*, and *Lady Knight*. At that time, her publishers limited the length of her books to 200 manuscript pages, thinking children would not want to read anything longer.

While writing the first book, Tammy found that because

Did you know...

Most of Tamora Pierce's books have a map at the beginning. "I cannot live without maps," she said. "When I'm writing I always start with a map, because I don't know where I am if I don't have one that I work on concurrently with the text."* But she also has no notion of scale. So when she has finished a book, she sends the map to a friend in California, Rick Robinson, with notes as to how long it takes the characters to ride, walk, or even, in the case of *Coldfire*, skate from point A to point B. He will then remake the map to scale.

Tammy has several atlases, a file drawer full of printed maps from around the world, and another drawer full of single-sheet maps she has clipped from *National Geographic* and other magazines. When she is creating a new universe for a book, she can design fictional cities and countries based on these maps. Maps are also the source for many of the names in her books. She said:

If I'm building on a culture from our real world, I can go into a detailed map of that area and pull out chunks of obscure place names and work with those. I end up with names for places and people's last names that sound like they came from a real language, because they did.**

* Donna Dailey's interviews with Tamora Pierce, May–July 2005.

** Ibid.

everyone knew Kel was a girl, she faced many more problems as a page than Alanna, who had saved herself a good deal of grief by pretending to be a boy—although she ran into other difficulties. By the time she got to page 180, Tammy had not finished Kel's first year. With her deadline approaching, rather than cut a lot of material she felt was good, she and Tim put their heads together and came up with the idea of Kel's probation, giving her a reason to split the book into two. Once more, Tammy had a quartet, which she would call The Protector of the Small.

With Alanna, Tammy had done what many first-time writers do: she tried to get everything in because she might not get another chance. So she made Alanna both a mage and a knight. She felt she had not done justice to either. Since then she had written plenty of mage characters. Now she wanted to concentrate on a knight, and she thought it would be a challenge to create a heroine who had no magic.

Kel would be very different from Alanna. Whereas Alanna was small and had speed going for her, as a big girl Kel's skills were going to be very different. She would be more centered, and her nature would reflect that. She also needed a different weapon specialty. Tammy decided this would be a good time to pull in her knowledge of samurai Japan, and give Kel those skills and temperament to fall back on via her Yamani background. Kel is more easy-going than Alanna. And Mallory suggested that instead of making her a loner, like Tammy's other heroes, she should be a natural commander.

Bringing Kel along as a commander in a setting where not everyone was going to like her was tricky. Tammy had been reading military history for decades, and she enjoyed bringing that into the story. She also wrote in her first functioning family, a family with a good mother, which was another stretch for her.

Developing Kel's relationship with her maid, Lalasa, was important. Tammy had to be careful not to neglect Kel's feminine side, or she would not come across as a complete character. Having Neal in the mix was great fun, because where Kel makes the best of things, Neal does not have to be nice. He says what everyone is thinking. They made a good pairing.

But the character Tammy is most proud of is Kel's training master, Lord Wyldon. She said:

> He could so easily have been a one-note character when I started out. He might as well have had a cape and a moustache. I was having trouble writing him, until Tim pointed out that I wouldn't be happy with a character like that. I needed to find something I liked about him. Wyldon turned into a character with more facets to him, and I love the way his relationship with Kel developed.[50]

In 1998, Tammy went to London, England. It was the first time she had enough money to travel outside the continental United States. After meeting her United Kingdom publisher and visiting a girl's school, she walked and walked all over the city. She had tea at the Ritz and went to Hatchard's bookstore. And after reading and writing about them for so many years, at the Tower of London Tammy put her hands on real medieval fortifications for the first time.

As a now-famous author, Tamora Pierce travels extensively. She hosts book signings, makes author appearances, and visits schools across the United States and Europe. This 1999 photo was Tammy's second author publicity photo.

10

On Tour

FIRST TEST WAS PUBLISHED in May 1999, and *Page* came out the following year. Alongside the Kel books, *Magic Steps*, the first in The Circle Opens quartet, came out in March 2000. To promote the new series, Scholastic Ltd. in London brought Tammy back to England in May on her first publisher-sponsored tour.

It was a whirlwind trip, taking her to libraries, schools, and bookstores from the south to the north of England and on into Scotland. "When you start your imaginative life with Robin Hood, it's sort of a dream date," Tammy said.[51]

She asked if she could take the train, rather than fly, from

Lancashire to Edinburgh so that she could see a bit of the countryside. As the train pulled into Edinburgh's central station, she looked up and saw Edinburgh Castle high atop the escarpment. In the taxi, Tammy stared at it out the back window and burst into tears.

She assured her worried companion that they were happy tears. "I'm at my second favorite fortification in the world," she exclaimed, "and I wrote my way here!"[52] Her tight schedule allowed just enough time for a photo at the castle gates the next morning. Then she was off for a rapid-fire tour of Oxford before flying home.

2000 was also the year in which Listening Library began to publish The Song of the Lioness quartet as single reader audio books. Tammy even got to meet Trini Alvarado, who looks so much like her conception of Daine, and to watch her record. From the Song of the Lioness quartet, Listening Library would quickly move on to other Tortall stories.

Street Magic, the next book in The Circle Opens series, was published in March 2001. The third Kel book, *Squire*, came out in June. *Squire* made the top 10 on the *New York Times* children's bestseller list for two weeks running. Tammy said:

> *Squire* was the hardest book I ever had to end. Even though I was late on the deadline, I put off finishing it for a week because I so enjoyed the relationship between Kel and her knight master, Raoul of Goldenlake, and I knew it would be a long time before I could come back to that. I really liked the way they worked together.[53]

Raoul, who first appeared in the Lioness books, was modeled after a friend of hers from college named Rick. Commander Buri, who becomes Raoul's girlfriend in *Squire*, was based on one of Tammy's girls from the group home. Kel's relationships with her boyfriend Cleon and training master Lord Wyldon also progress in this book.

Tammy and fellow writer, Meg Cabot, author of *The Princess Diaries*, met in June, 2001. They talked about how hard it had been to find female heroes when they were growing up. They decided to start a discussion website where users could share information about women they admire, voice their opinions, and chat about topics from current events and entertainment to homework. They thrashed out the main forum and the subjects, Tim designed the website, and Meg suggested the title "Sheroes." The website launched that month, and by the end of the year they had 500 members. Today Sheroes Central has over 5,000 members around the world, aged 10 to 60. There is also a spin-off site, Sheroes Fans.

Soon after, Tammy was off on tour again, this time to Australia. She attended the Reading Matters Conference in Melbourne. She appeared at schools and bookstores both there and in Sydney for Scholastic. Tammy's Australian publisher took her to a zoo, where she could feed emus and kangaroos and pet a koala bear. She met Australian authors, and shipped home a box full of books.

Tammy returned to New York to work on her next book, *Lady Knight*. On September 10, 2001, she closed a chapter where Kel reports to Lord Wyldon on the state of things at the refugee camp where Kel is in command. The next morning, on September 11, terrorists flew airplanes into the World Trade Center.

From their apartment on 91st Street and Broadway, Tammy and Tim watched the television in horror as the Twin Towers collapsed. They called their friend Raquel, who lived close enough to the Towers to walk outside and see them. She came back to the phone crying. Only two weeks earlier, she and Tammy had been shopping in the World Trade Center on the concourse level.

Outside Tammy's apartment, there was no traffic on Broadway, only an eerie quiet as people in business suits walked north in silence. After a while, Tammy and Tim could not stand being inside anymore. They decided to go for a walk in Riverside Park. Along the streets, they saw people sitting outside on their stoops, talking quietly. The stores were jammed full with people stocking up on groceries. Tammy spent most of the afternoon and evening contacting family and friends by email and through the website, assuring everyone she was OK.

Tammy was proud of her fellow New Yorkers and their generous response to the disaster, donating money, blood, sweat, and tears. She had often heard disparaging remarks about the city and New Yorkers in general, and she hoped that people would see and remember what New Yorkers are really like, regardless of how they may appear. Her next two books, *Cold Fire* and *Lady Knight*, carried dedications to the people of New York and to the fire fighters, police, rescue workers, and medical personnel.

After September 11, all Tammy wanted to do was get back to Tortall. She forgot that in the next chapter, Kel returns to find the camp has been attacked and she must search the rubble for the dead. It was really hard to write that scene.

Tammy was scheduled to do a major U.S. tour for Random House. Her publisher called to ask if she wanted to cancel it or make it shorter. Tammy said no, because if she did that, the terrorists would have won. Her American fans had been waiting to meet her for years, and she was not going to disappoint them. She trusted that security would be in place.

It certainly was. Tammy went out on tour in October. At

each airport she was searched and searched and searched. Once she was even taken off the plane to be searched. She was livid until she found out that all the writers on tour were getting the same treatment. It was because they had one-way tickets, going from one city to the next. One-way ticketing was the considered to be a sign of a possible terrorist on airplanes at that time. Tammy carried on with the tour, submitting to the delays as best she could.

In just three weeks, she traveled from coast to coast, beginning in the Seattle area. She spoke in over 30 schools, bookstores, and other venues in multiple cities in California, Texas, Minnesota, Illinois, Ohio, Virginia, New Jersey, Pennsylvania, Massachusetts, and New York. In San Jose, California, she saw her father for what would be the last time.

One night in St. Paul, Minnesota, she read from *Cold Fire* (the third book in The Circle Opens quartet), which would be published in March. During a scene where Daja enters a burning building to rescue a blind girl, Tammy almost broke down on stage, remembering September 11. After a break, she continued with a five-city tour across Canada at the end of November.

In February, at the Boskone science fiction conventions, Tammy often found herself on the same panels with the best-selling children's author Bruce Coville. Over time they became good friends. In 2000, Bruce had asked Tammy to contribute to a new anthology he was editing, called *Half Human*. She wrote a story called "Elder Brother," about a tree that was turned into a man due to an event that took place in *Wolf-Speaker*. *Half Human* was published in 2001.

Previously, Bruce had been a producer of audio books for the Listening Library. He missed doing it, and was thinking

As an accomplished writer, wife, and world traveler, Tamora Pierce could not be any happier with her life. She can escape to fantasy lands through reading or writing and she brings readers with her. Here we see Tammy at a 2003 bookstore appearance in La Jolla, California.

of starting his own audio company. He approached Tammy about recording her Circle of Magic books. Tammy encouraged him by saying she thought he would be perfect reading as Niko.

In February 2002, Tammy and Tim drove to Syracuse, New York, to record *Sandry's Book* with Bruce's new company, Full Cast Audio. Tammy was the narrator. Tim took on the difficult role of Dedicate Crane. And Bruce, of course, was Niko. There were 23 actors in all, juggling 50 speaking parts, and the roles of Sandry, Daja, Tris, and Briar were played by local kids and teenagers.

Tammy was thrilled, if a little nervous, to be back in front of a microphone again. It was wonderful to hear her characters brought to life by a group of good actors who worked hard to make them vivid and real. She watched their faces light up as they read or listened to what she had written, and saw their deep concentration during dramatic scenes that touched on their own experiences. She said:

> Full Cast Audio erased my last questions about what I had achieved. I had created something of value, something that other busy, talented people thought was worth the time and labor and expense to perform. I was telling real stories about real lives.[54]

It was a gift she would never forget.

Recordings of *Tris's Book* and *Daja's Book* followed in 2003, with *Briar's Book* in 2004. They went on to record *Wild Magic* and, in 2005, *Street Magic*. *Will of the Empress* is also slated for recording, as is *Melting Stones*, a new story Tammy wrote specially with the actors in mind. This "book" will be recorded by the audio company before it appears in print.

After enjoying four-star hotels on tour, Tammy found it hard to return to their cramped studio apartment. In April 2002, she and Tim moved to a much bigger, two-bedroom apartment. It was just two blocks away, on the 19th floor with views over the Central Park Reservoir and midtown Manhattan. The spare room became Tammy's office, and she loved having all her reference books and materials around her in one place. From her window she could see cormorants, egrets, crows, seagulls, and even the occasional red-tailed hawk or peregrine falcon. To celebrate the move, Tammy and Tim got a new cat, Gremlin, to help fill their new space. Gremlin joined their current family of three cats—Scrap, Pee Wee, and Scooter—and two parakeets—Timon and Egg.

Did you know...

For 17 years, Tamora Pierce wrote in her living room. Now she has an office where she also keeps her substantial reference library. A large part of her collection is made up of children's reference books. "Kid's books have so many more pictures than adult books," she said, "and I need actual pictures. I realized I could not envision things from words, such as the size of dinosaur skeletons, if I wasn't familiar with them."* While writing *The Emperor Mage*, she found a children's book that had pictures of different dinosaurs next to a bus, an airplane, or a human being, and has used children's books ever since.

Tammy has two shelves full of travel guides to different parts of the world. One bookshelf is full of dictionaries and phrase books in different languages so she can cobble new languages together. Another shelf is full of baby name books. "I used to really struggle with character names until someone recommended a book of New Age baby names, which was full of unusual names," she said.** Rounding out the collection are cookbooks and architecture books, as well as her files full of maps and photos.

* Donna Dailey's interviews with Tamora Pierce, May–July 2005.

** Ibid.

In September 2002, the final Kel book, *Lady Knight*, debuted at number one on the *New York Times* children's best seller list. And on the *Wall Street Journal* bestseller list, which includes adult and children's fiction, it was listed as number six. Tammy was so surprised she sat down right on the floor when she heard the news.[55]

The only thing to mar her happiness was that her father was not around to celebrate with her. Wayne had died in March, after a long battle with obstructive pulmonary disease (a disease of the airways that slowly leads to loss of lung function often caused by smoking[56]). It had been hard for Tammy to see him tethered to an oxygen tank after a life of riding motorcycles, fishing, and being in the great outdoors. She dedicated her next book, *Shatterglass* (the fourth and final book in The Circle Opens quartet), which came out in March 2003, to him with the words: "You taught me to soar with my stories. Now, at last, the Old Eagle flies free. May you find good winds, clean air, and the universe under your wings."[57] With her stepmother, stepbrothers, and her sister Kim, Tammy misses him and she will always be grateful to him for the gift of writing.

Tammy received more and more invitations to speak at conferences, schools, and libraries. She was sponsored for more tours as well. Every autumn for the next three years she went on author tours in the United States, and sometimes Canada as well, for Random House. In October 2003 Tammy returned to Australia for the Island Journeys Conference in Hobart, Tasmania. This time Tim came with her. They also visited Sydney and Melbourne on a promotional tour for Scholastic in Australia. In 2004 and 2005, Scholastic Press sent her on U.S. tours.

Song of the Lioness series fans had long awaited a story about Alanna's daughter, Aly, and in 2002 Tammy started writing *Trickster's Choice*. Instead of following in her famous mother's footsteps, Aly wants to be a spy, like her father, much to her parents' dismay. Aly gets her chance when she is kidnapped by pirates and taken to the Copper Isles. There she makes a wager with the trickster god Kyprioth in order to get home. The book came out in the fall of 2003, and was followed by *Trickster's Queen* a year later.

Kyprioth was modeled on her friend Bruce Coville, but Aly was a challenging character for Tammy. By nature, spies are quiet people who stay in the background and do not draw attention to themselves. For Aly to succeed as a character, Tammy had to find alternatives for the lively fight scenes she was used to writing. She said:

> The Trickster books were the hardest thing I've ever done. There were so many layers to keep track of, so many characters to keep up with. I had at least four different conspiracies to deal with at any one time.[58]

In addition to the complicated plot, Tammy was traveling a lot during the writing of both books.

The scramble was worth it. The Trickster books brought in a whole new audience over the age of 15 for the first time. Tammy began to see three generations—daughters, mothers, and grandmothers—showing up at her appearances. *Trickster's Queen* debuted at number one on the *New York Times* children's best seller list, and stayed on the list for seven weeks.

With *Squire*, Tammy's publishers had finally taken her off the 200 pages per book limit, and she could break away from writing quartets. "Everybody assumed there was a great mystical meaning between me and quartets," she said. "It was just that it took me 800 pages to tell my average story of one person creating her life."[59]

The two Trickster books are about 850 pages in total. For her next Circle book, *The Will of the Empress*, published in October 2005, she only needed 500 pages to tell the story of Sandry, Tris, Daja, and Briar coming back together again as 18-year-olds. Together they visit Sandry's relatives in Namorn where they encounter a willful empress who wants to keep them there. Their fans finally saw some of them deal with romance, which they had clamored for. The book was also unusual in that there are no battlefield casualties, something unheard-of in a Tamora Pierce book!

Tammy has several novels planned that will take her up to 2010. A new trilogy, set 200 years before the time of the Song of the Lioness series, will tell the story of Rebekah Cooper, whose only desire is to become a Provost's Guard. Known as Beka, she is the ancestor of George Cooper—Alanna's husband and Aly's father.

After that, Tammy's next two books for Random House will be stand-alone novels. One will be about the mage Numair Salmalín and his adventures between leaving Carthak and meeting Daine. Another will be about Maura of Dunlath, the child from *Wolf-Speaker*, and how she finds her place in the world. And there will be two more Circle books for Scholastic.

When those books are completed, Tammy would like to take a year off. Even her most avid readers would have to agree she deserves it. But somehow, you get the feeling, it might just depend on what is happening in Tortall.

1 Donna Dailey's interviews with Tamora Pierce, May–July 2005.

2 Ibid.

3 Ibid.

4 Tim Podell, *Good Conversations: A Talk With Tamora Pierce* (Scarborough, NY: Tim Podell Productions, 2004).

5 Laura T. Ryan, "World of Magic and Mysticism," *The Post-Standard/Stars*, January 2003.

6 Donald R. Gallo, ed. *Speaking for Ourselves, Too: More Autobiographical Sketches by Notable Authors of Books for Young Adults* (Urbana, IL: National Council of Teachers of English, 1993).

7 Donna Dailey's interviews with Tamora Pierce, May–July 2005.

8 Ibid.

9 Ibid.

10 Ibid.

11 Ibid.

12 Ibid.

13 Ibid.

14 Ibid.

15 Ibid.

16 Ibid.

7 Ibid.

18 Ibid.

19 Ibid.

20 Ibid.

21 Ibid.

22 Ibid.

23 Ibid.

24 Ibid.

25 Ibid.

26 Ibid.

27 Ibid.

28 Ibid.

29 Ibid.

30 Ibid.

31 Ibid.

32 Ibid.

33 Ibid.

34 Ibid.

35 Ibid.

36 Ibid.

37 Ibid.

38 Ibid.

39 Ibid.

40 Ibid.

41 Ibid.

42 Ibid.

43 Ibid.

44 Ibid.

45 Ibid.

46 Ibid.

47 Ibid.

48 Ibid.

49 Ibid.

50 Ibid.

51 Ibid.

52 Ibid.

53 Ibid.

54 Tamora Pierce, "Tamora Pierce Biography: Personal Sketches," Second Bio Page—about working with Full Cast Audio, *www.tamora-pierce.com/bio2.htm*.

55 Donna Dailey's interviews with

Tamora Pierce, May–July 2005.

56 National Heart, Lung, and Blood Institute, "Chronic Obstructive Pulmonary Disease, NIH publication No. 03-5229, March 2003, *www.nhlbi.nih.gov/health/public/lung/other/copd_fact.pdf.*

57 Donna Dailey's interviews with Tamora Pierce, May–July 2005.

58 Ibid.

59 Ibid.

1954 Tamora (Tammy) Pierce is born on December 13 in South Connellsville, Pennsylvania, to Wayne Franklin Pierce and Jacqueline (Jackie) Sparks Pierce.

1960 The family moves to Dunbar. Tammy's younger sister Kimberly (Kim) Pierce is born.

1961 Youngest sister Melanie Pierce is born.

1963 The Pierce family moves to California, near San Francisco. Over the next two years, they move several times before settling in Burlingame, California, where Tammy attends sixth grade. Wayne hears her telling herself stories and encourages her to start writing them down.

1966 Tammy writes stories to block out her parents' marital problems. Wayne moves out on Mother's Day. Tammy's seventh grade teacher introduces her to J.R.R. Tolkien's Lord of the Rings trilogy and she becomes hooked on fantasy novels.

1968 Tammy's mother moves the family back to Pennsylvania. As Jackie's drinking worsens, they move from Uniontown to rural Smithfield. After an argument with her mother, Tammy loses the ability to write her own fiction stories.

1971 The family moves back to Uniontown for Tammy's senior year in high school. She writes a humorous column for the school newspaper and acts in school plays. She dates a college boy who becomes the model for the character of Duke Roger in her first novel.

1972 Tammy enrolls in the University of Pennsylvania in Philadelphia, Pennsylvania. She becomes a psychology major and meets Jay Levine, who is her boyfriend for the next five and a half years.

1975 In her junior year, Tammy breaks through her writer's block and writes her first story in five years. In May she makes her first sale to Intimate Story magazine.

1976 In her senior year, Tammy takes a fiction writing course. In June, she completes her first novel. She gets her bachelor's degree in August and moves to Kingston, New York.

1977 In March, Tammy finishes *The Song of the Lioness*, a novel written for adults. She and Jay break up.

1978 Tammy moves to Buhl, Idaho, in August to renew her ties with her father and stepmother, Mary Lou. She gets a job as house mother at a group home for girls. She reads her novel out loud to the girls, editing it as she goes for her teenage listeners.

1979 In August, Tammy moves to New York City to pursue her writing career. She writes film reviews for martial arts magazines. In October she begins a job as an office assistant at the Harold Ober literary agency.

1980 Tammy shows *The Song of the Lioness* to Claire Smith at the Harold Ober literary agency. Claire becomes her first agent; she suggests Tammy turn her novel into four books for teenagers.

1981 Tammy meets with Jean Karl at Atheneum Books, who agrees to publish the quartet after some revision. In her spare time, Tammy helps start an amateur radio company and writes radio plays.

1982 Tammy and her associates turn the amateur radio company into the professional radio company, ZPPR. She meets Tim Liebe, who joins the company as an actor, writer, and director.

1983 *Alanna: The First Adventure*, the first book in the Song of the Lioness series, is published by Atheneum Books in hardcover in September. Tammy leaves her job at the literary agency to concentrate on writing. She works as a temporary secretary to make ends meet.

1984 *In the Hand of the Goddess*, the second book in the Song of the Lioness series, is published.

1985 Tammy sells her first fantasy short story, "Plain Magic," to Oxford University Press in England. She takes a secretarial job at Chase Manhattan Bank. Marries Tim Liebe.

1986 The third book in the Song of the Lioness series, *The Woman Who Rides Like a Man*, is published.

1988 *Lioness Rampant*, the final book in the Song of the Lioness series is published. Tammy leaves ZPPR; she continues writing and works at various full- and part-time secretarial jobs to make ends meet.

1992 *Wild Magic* is published, the first of a new series called The Immortals. With more royalties coming in from overseas sales, she quits secretarial work and begins writing full time.

1993 Tammy's mother dies in a state institution of Huntington's Chorea.

1994 *Wolf-Speaker* (The Immortals) is published.

1995 *The Emperor Mage* (The Immortals) is published. Tammy makes her first speaking tour, in the San Francisco Bay Area.

1996 *Realms of the Gods* (The Immortals) is published. Tammy moves to a new publisher, Scholastic, for her next series, The Circle of Magic.

1997 *Sandry's Book*, the first book in The Circle of Magic series, is published. Random House re-issues the The Song of the Lioness and The Immortals quartets in paperback.

1998 The second and third books in The Circle of Magic series, *Tris's Book* and *Daja's Book*, are published. Tammy visits London on her first overseas trip.

1999 The publication of *Briar's Book* completes The Circle of Magic quartet. Tammy agrees to write a new series, The Circle Opens, for Scholastic, and a new Tortall adventure series The Protector of the Small, for Random House. *First Test*, the first book in The Protector of the Small series is published.

2000 *Magic Steps* (The Circle Opens) and *Page* (The Protector of the Small) are published. Tammy goes to England on her first publisher-sponsored tour for Scholastic.

2001 *Street Magic* (The Circle Opens) and *Squire* (Protector of the Small) are published. Tammy founds the Sheroes Central website with author Meg Cabot. She travels to Australia and around the United States and Canada on book tours. A fantasy short story, "Elder Brother," is published.

2002 *Cold Fire* (The Circle Opens) is published. Tammy records *Sandry's Book* as an audio book with Bruce Coville's Full Cast Audio company. *Lady Knight* (The Protector of the Small) debuts at number one on the *New York Times* children's bestseller list. Tammy's father dies after a long illness.

2003 *Shatterglass* (The Circle Opens) is published. *Tris's Book* and *Daja's Book* are recorded with Full Cast Audio. *Trickster's Choice* is published in the fall.

2004 *Briar's Book* and *Wild Magic* are recorded with Full Cast Audio. *Trickster's Queen* is published.

2005 *Street Magic* is recorded with Full Cast Audio. *The Will of the Empress* is published. Tammy co-edits an anthology, *Young Warriors*.

SONG OF THE LIONESS QUARTET

These four books tell the story of Alanna of Trebond and how she became a respected knight. Alanna wants to become a knight in the kingdom of Tortall at a time when girls are forbidden to be warriors. In *Alanna: The First Adventure*, Alanna trades places with her twin brother Thom, disguising herself as a boy to begin training at the palace. As she struggles to achieve her goals, she becomes close friends with the heir to the throne, Prince Jonathan, and with George Cooper, the King of Thieves. She also meets a powerful enemy, Duke Roger. In the second book, *In the Hand of the Goddess*, Alanna sees battle as Jonathan's squire and reveals her secret during a deadly duel. Now a lady knight, Alanna seeks adventure among the desert tribes in *The Woman Who Rides Like a Man*. In the final book, *Lioness Rampant*, Alanna embarks on a quest to find the Dominion Jewel, a legendary gem which can save Tortall from destruction when her nemesis returns from the dead.

THE IMMORTALS QUARTET

In *Wild Magic*, orphaned Daine gets a job helping the royal horse mistress in Tortall. There she discovers her knack with animals is a rare kind of magic. She finds friends and a teacher, the great mage Numair, as the world is invaded by immortal creatures bent on destruction. In *Wolf-Speaker*, Daine strengthens her magical bond with animals when she and her companions go to the aid of a wolf pack and discover a dark plot which threatens the kingdom. As Daine grows into her power in *The Emperor Mage*, she sails to Carthak for a peace conference with the power-mad Emperor Ozorne, whose evil spells have unleashed the Immortals, but she finds the gods have chosen her to deliver retribution to the Emperor Mage. In *Realms of the Gods*, Ozorne has formed an alliance with the god of Chaos in a fierce battle to destroy Tortall, and Daine travels to the Divine Realms where she discovers the secret of her strange parentage.

THE CIRCLE OF MAGIC QUARTET

In this series, which is set in a new world, Emelan, the lives of four unusual young mages—Sandry, Tris, Daja, and Briar—are interwoven through magic and friendship. Orphaned or abandoned by their families, they struggle to come to terms with their backgrounds and their magical gifts at the temple city of Winding Circle. Though each book is named for, and centers on, one of the four, their adventures are bound tightly together.

THE PROTECTOR OF THE SMALL QUARTET

Keladry of Mindelan is determined to follow in the footsteps of her hero, Alanna the Lioness, and become a knight of Tortall. But the palace training master, Lord Wyldon, does not believe a girl should train in combat arts. Neither do many of Kel's fellow pages. *First Test* is the story of Kel's probationary year as she struggles to prove she is equal to the boys. In *Page*, Kel continues her training as her enemies plot to drive her away from the palace. *Squire* follows Kel through four years of service to her knight-master, Raoul of Goldenlake, one of Alanna's oldest friends and a true warrior. Raoul helps Kel hone her skills as she approaches her final test in the Chamber of the Ordeal. In *Lady Knight*, Tortall is at war and Kel is put in charge of a refugee camp, preventing her from pursuing the task set for her by the Chamber: to find and destroy an evil mage and his monstrous killing devices.

TRICKSTER'S CHOICE AND TRICKSTER'S QUEEN

These two books tell the story of Alanna's 16-year-old daughter, Aly. Her parents refuse to sanction her chosen career as a spy, but she gets her chance when she is kidnapped by pirates and taken to the Copper Isles, where she makes an unusual bargain with the trickster god Kyprioth in order to earn her freedom.

1983 *Alanna: The First Adventure* (Song of the Lioness)

1984 *In the Hand of the Goddess* (Song of the Lioness)

1986 *The Woman Who Rides Like a Man* (Song of the Lioness)

1988 *Lioness Rampant* (Song of the Lioness)

1992 *Wild Magic* (The Immortals)

1994 *Wolf-Speaker* (The Immortals)

1995 *The Emperor Mage* (The Immortals)

1996 *Realms of the Gods* (The Immortals)

1997 *Sandry's Book* (The Circle of Magic)

1998 *Tris's Book* (The Circle of Magic), *Daja's Book* (The Circle of Magic)

1999 *Briar's Book* (The Circle of Magic), *First Test* (The Protector of the Small)

2000 *Page* (The Protector of the Small), *Magic Steps* (The Circle Opens)

2001 *Squire* (The Protector of the Small), *Street Magic* (The Circle Opens)

2002 *Lady Knight* (The Protector of the Small), *Cold Fire* (The Circle Opens)

2003 *Shatterglass* (The Circle Opens), *Trickster's Choice*

2004 *Trickster's Queen*

2005 *The Will of the Empress*

AUDIO BOOKS

2000 *Alanna: The First Adventure*

2001 *In the Hand of the Goddess*

2002 *Lioness Rampant, The Woman Who Rides Like a Man, Sandry's Book*

2003 *Tris's Book, Daja's Book, Trickster's Choice*

2004 *Briar's Book, Wild Magic, Trickster's Queen*

2005 *Street Magic*

OTHER WORKS

1986 "Plain Magic," short story in *Planetfall*, Douglas Hill ed.

1993 "Fantasy: Why Kids Read It, Why Kids Need It," from *School Library Journal*, reprinted in *Only Connect: Readings in Children's Literature*, Sheila Egoff et ors. ed.

1999 "Plain Magic," short story in *Flights of Fantasy*, Perfection Learning.

2001 "Elder Brother," short story in *Half Human*, anthology, Bruce Coville, ed.; "Testing," short story in *Lost and Found*, Helen and M. Jerry Weiss, ed.

2004 "Plain Magic," short story in literature textbook, Brigham Young University; "The Case of Folquin's Folly," minute mystery, Disney Adventures.

2005 *Young Warriors*, anthology, Tamora Pierce and Josepha Sherman, ed.; "Student of Ostriches," short story in *Young Warriors*.

2006 "Time of Proving," short story in Cricket magazine; "Huntress," short story in *Firebirds Rising*, Sharyn November, ed.; "The Hidden Girl," short story in *Visions and Dreams*, Helen and M. Jerry Weiss, ed.

ALANNA OF TREBOND

The heroine of the Song of the Lioness series, Alanna of Trebond is a stubborn girl with copper-colored hair and violet eyes. She is so determined to become a knight that she disguises herself as a boy until she wins her shield. As a warrior and a mage, she becomes a legend in her time and is known as the Lioness.

THOM OF TREBOND

Alanna's twin brother, Thom wants to become a sorcerer, not a knight, and so he agrees to trade places with his sister. He goes in her place to the convent where he learns to become a master sorcerer. It is he who brings Alanna's greatest enemy back to life in order to prove his power.

JONATHAN OF CONTÉ

Prince Jonathan of Conté, the heir to the throne, is Alanna's friend and first love. He is handsome, with dark hair and sapphire eyes, loyal and proud. He becomes King of Tortall.

GEORGE COOPER

The King of the Thieves, George befriends Alanna and her noble friends, and teaches them the ways of the lower city. Jonathan rewards George's loyalty by making him a baron and confidential agent. George falls in love with Alanna and patiently wins her hand with his sense of humor and easy-going charm.

DUKE ROGER

Jonathan's handsome and charming cousin is a powerful sorcerer with secret ambitions to seize the throne. Alanna manages to kill him in a duel, but her brother Thom brings him back from the dead and he nearly destroys Tortall.

SIR MYLES OF OLAU

Sir Myles of Olau is the wise and kindly knight who takes Alanna under his wing. He is a historian and spymaster. He eventually makes her his adopted daughter and heir.

THAYET JIAN WILIMA

The beautiful daughter of a Saren warlord, exiled-princess Thayet is both independent minded and skilled in courtly behavior. She becomes Jonathan's wife and Queen of Tortall.

RAOUL OF GOLDENLAKE

Alanna and Jonathan's friend during their years as pages and squires, Raoul becomes the Knight Commander of the King's Own. In *Squire*, he becomes Keladry of Mindelan's knight-master.

DAINE

The heroine of The Immortals series. The orphan Daine is the daughter of a human mother and a minor god of the hunt, Weiryn. With her special powers of wild magic, she can talk to animals and even transform herself into their shape. Her magic and her devotion to her new friends help to save Tortall when the world is invaded by creatures from the immortal realms.

NUMAIR SALMALÍN

Daine's tall, lanky teacher is a scholar and the greatest mage in Tortall. As he helps her discover her magical gifts, he becomes her friend and in the end they fall in love.

KELADRY OF MINDELAN

The heroine of The Protector of the Small series, Kel is a big, strong girl who dreams of becoming a knight like the Lioness. Although she has no magic, she has excellent combat skills and the temperament to succeed against all odds. As she hones her warrior skills she proves herself to be a natural commander.

NEAL OF QUEENSCOVE

Kel's best friend is the son of Duke Baird, the royal healer. He has a wicked tongue and an irreverence for authority that disguise his sense of fairness and loyalty.

LORD WYLDON OF CAVALL

Kel's training master seems, at first, harsh and inflexible. He makes life as difficult as possible in order to dissuade her from becoming a knight, but as she proves herself he comes to respect her and value her skills.

ALIANNE (ALY)

The heroine of *Trickster's Choice* and *Trickster's Queen*. The daughter of Alanna and George Cooper, she has her mother's determination and her father's skills as a spy. She discovers a few special talents of her own in her adventures in the Copper Isles.

SANDRY

One of the four heroes of the two Circle series, Lady Sandrilene fa Toren is a noble whose parents have died of smallpox. Her thread magic weaves the powers of her three friends into a powerful bond.

TRIS

Trisana Chandler, another of the four heroes of the two Circle series, is a merchant's daughter whose family have abandoned her.

With her teacher Niklaren (Niko) Goldeye, she learns to control her powerful magic, which works with the forces of wind, earth, water, and storms.

DAJA

Daja Kisubo is a Trader who survives a shipwreck which kills her family, only to be cast out from Trader life for bringing bad luck. As one of the four Circle heroes, she learns to work magic through working metals with her teacher, Frostpine.

BRIAR

Briar Moss is a street rat and convicted thief, who is rescued by Niko and brought to the temple city. With his three Circle companions and the help of his teacher Rosethorn, he learns to master his magical gift with plants.

1984 *Alanna: The First Adventure* won an Author's Citation from The Alumni Association, New Jersey Institute of Technology, 17th Annual New Jersey Writers Conference.

1985–6 *In the Hand of the Goddess* won the ZDF Preis der Lesratten (German fantasy award) and was nominated for the South Carolina Children's Book Award.

1998 The Circle of Magic: *Sandry's Book* was named the Honor Book in the Judy Lopez Memorial Award of the Women's National Book Association.

1999 The Circle of Magic: *Tris's Book* was named on the Quick Pick for Reluctant Young Adult Readers list, YALSA (Young Adult Library Services Association).

2000 *Page* made the *New York Times* Children's Chapter Book best-seller list and *VOYA/Voice of Youth Advocates* magazine's Best Science Fiction, Fantasy, and Horror List.

2001 *Squire* made the *New York Times* Children's Chapter Book best-seller list for two consecutive weeks in June, as well as *VOYA/Voice of Youth Advocates* magazine's Best Science Fiction, Fantasy, and Horror List.

2002 *Lady Knight* debuted at number one on the *New York Times* Children's Chapter Book bestseller list and remained on the list for three weeks; at the same time, it made number six and 12 con-secutively on the *Wall Street Journal* Fiction bestseller list. The book was also rated highly on the *Publisher's Weekly* Children's Chapter Book bestseller list. Both *Lady Knight* and *Cold Fire* made the Amazon Online Best Teen Books of 2002 list.

2003 *Trickster's Choice* made the *New York Times* Children's Chapter Book bestseller list, and the American Library Association's Best Books for Young Adults List.

2004–5 *Trickster's Queen* debuted at number one on the *New York Times* Children's Chapter Book bestseller list and stayed on the list for seven weeks. In 2005 it won the Edward E. Smith Memorial "Skylark" Award at Boskone 42.

Tamora Pierce's books have consistently appeared on many "best lists" for children's books, including the following: Best Books for Young Adults List, the American Library Association; Books for the Teen Age list, Office of Young Adult Services of The New York Public Library; *VOYA/Voice of Youth Advocates* magazine's Best Science Fiction, Fantasy, and Horror List, as well as *VOYA*'s Top Shelf for Middle School Readers list; Recommended Fantasy of "GenreCon" (the Preconference on Genres of the Young Adult Services Division of the American Librarians Association, June 1991); Iowa Children's Choice Award Master List.

Bennett, Steve. "Trickster's author to make San Antonio stop at Twig." *San Antonio Express-News*, September 2004. *www.mysanantonio.com/salife/stories/MYSA091304.14P.book_pierce.6da460fc.html.*

Crocker, Kellye Carter. "Strong 'sheroes' no longer fantasy." *Des Moines Register*, October 20, 2004. *http://desmoinesregister.com/apps/pbcs.dll/article?AID=/20041020/NEWS08/410200302/1001/NEWS.*

Gallo, Donald R., ed. *Speaking for Ourselves, Too: More Autobiographical Sketches by Notable Authors of Books for Young Adults* (Urbana, IL: National Council of Teachers of English, 1993).

National Heart, Lung, and Blood Institute, "Chronic Obstructive Pulmonary Disease, NIH publication No. 03-5229, March 2003, *www.nhlbi.nih.gov/health/public/lung/other/copd_fact.pdf.*

Pierce, Tamora. "Tamora Pierce Biography: Personal Sketches," Second Bio Page—about working with Full Cast Audio, *www.tamora-pierce.com/bio2.htm.*

————. Tamora Pierce's Official Website, *www.tamorapierce.com.*

Podell, Tim. *Good Conversations: A Talk With Tamora Pierce.* Scarborough, NY: Tim Podell Productions, 2004.

Ryan, Laura T. "Worlds of Magic and Mysticism." *The Post-Standard/Stars*, January 2003.

Tillis, Vicki. "Area library, schools plan trip to see author." *Fairfield Ledger*, October 2004.

Brown, Joanne, and Nancy St. Clair, ed. *Declarations of Independence: Empowered Girls in Young Adult Literature, 1990–2001*. Lanham, MD: The Scarecrow Press, Inc., 2002.

Buxton, Richard. *The Complete World of Greek Mythology*. New York, NY: Thames & Hudson, 2004.

Lehr, Susan, ed. "Heroes for Children: Battling Good and Evil." From *Battling Dragons: Issues and Controversy in Children's Literature*. Portsmouth, NH: Heinemann, 1995.

Stewart, Mary. *The Crystal Cave*. New York, NY: William Morrow and Company, 1980.

Tolkein, J.R.R. *The Fellowship of the Ring*. Boston, MA: Houghton Mifflin, 1988.

White, T.H. *The Once and Future King*. New York, NY: Ace Edition under G.P. Putnam's Sons, 1987.

www.tamorapierce.com

This is Tamora Pierce's Official Website. It has a wealth of information about the author, her books and characters, frequently asked questions, upcoming publications, and a schedule of public appearances.

www.randomhouse.com/teens/tpierce.html

This is Random House Publisher's Children's Books Author's Spotlight on Tamora Pierce. It contains a short biography and overview of Tammy's books published by Random House.

www.scholastic.com

This is the website for Scholastic Inc., the publishing house who publishes Tamora Pierce's two Circle quartets: The Circle of Magic and The Circle Opens.

www.sheroescentral.com

This is a discussion board about female heroes set up by authors Tamora Pierce and Meg Cabot.

www.sheroesfans.com

This is a fan-moderated discussion board spun off from the Sheroes Central website.

www.steelsings.com

This is a website written by and for Tamora Pierce fans, with information on her books and characters. It also has access to role play games, chat rooms, and a fanzine (magazine written by and for fans especially of science fiction or fantasy writing).

www.teenreads.com/series/series-protector-author.asp

This is TeenReads.com's page about Tamora Pierce. It includes an interview with Pierce, a bibliography, trivia, and a list of her characters. The focus is exclusively on the Protector of the Small series.

www.authors4teens.com

This is the site of Don Gallo's interview with Tamora Pierce which was conducted on September 4, 2002. While this is a paid subscription site, a free trial is available.

page:

DONNA DAILEY is a journalist and author. She received a B.A. degree in Journalism from the University of Northern Colorado and later moved to London, England. She writes for magazines and newspapers worldwide, and has written more than twenty books and travel guides, including *Literary London* and Who Wrote That? *Charles Dickens.* She lives with her husband, the writer Mike Gerrard, in Arizona and in Cambridgeshire, England.